M. Mukhlesur Rahman Chowdhury

A Unique Military Intervention in Bangladesh

M. Mukhlesur Rahman Chowdhury

A Unique Military Intervention in Bangladesh

Dictus Publishing

Publisher:
Dictus Publishing
is a trademark of
International Book Market Service Ltd., member of OmniScriptum Publishing Group
17 Meldrum Street, Beau Bassin 71504, Mauritius
Printed at: see last page
ISBN: 978-3-8473-8591-2

Chapter 1

The Internationalisation Of Bangladeshi Military Intervention In 2007

By M Mukhlesur Rahman Chowdhury

17 November, 2014

International relations have major role in governing different countries, particularly, in this era of globalisation. It is more evident in developing countries' politics. Moreover, extra-constitutional government needs special support and attention from foreign powers for its legitimacy. Bangladesh witnessed military-backed government's parley to gain international support during its tenure of 2007-08 period. The military rule contacted relevant international powerful quarters in order to receive their supports.

Appointment of Dr. Fakhruddin Ahmed as the head of the government was nothing but first signal of military administration to show that they have international connections. On the one hand the military's priority was Dr. Muhammad Yunus, and on the other hand, Yunus's choice was different. He was more interested to be the head of the state or the President of the country. Instead of joining as head of the government or Chief Adviser during the army-backed regime Yunus made his all-out efforts to start with a journey for his new political front 'Nagarik Shakti'. However, that move has failed as people went against the military's anti-political behaviour.

Role of PR in UN

Initially, Permanent Representative of Bangladesh in United Nations Dr. Iftekhar Ahmed Chowdhury was aspirant for the position of the Chief Adviser. After completion of his regular appointment in the United Nations as Permanent Representative, Iftekhar was discharging his contractual assignment in the same position in New York. In fact, he was the unofficial adviser of Army Chief Moeen Uddin Ahmed prior to 11 January 2007 military coup.

Moeen was desperate to get international support for his takeover. Moeen and Iftekhar had series of meetings on the eve of '1/11' in New York where he managed a programme showing that he needed to visit UN Headquarters as Bangladesh is one of the major contributors in UN Peace Keeping Force where Bangladesh Army has been in leading position there. Iftekhar was highly ambitious in order for his elevation. Contrarily, Moeen was serious for Iftekhar as he thought sitting UN envoy may manoeuvre international body in favour of a military takeover. Thus, any possible sanctions against his military takeover can be avoided, as he thought. Iftekhar was saying 'Bangladesh needs a benevolent dictator' in 2005 while he was attending Halifax Conference in Canada. According to a Canadian journalist William Sloan, a coterie was working against democracy since then. A politician cum jurist Dr. Kamal Hossain also echoed in same voice and commented that they were trying to change the regime since 2005 against both BNP and Awami League.

Dr. Iftekhar A. Chowdhury wanted to be the United Nations Secretary General at the end of BNP regime, which was not possible to be implemented by the government as recently Bangladesh saw a major defeat in OIC Secretary General election. BNP government did not want to get another setback in diplomacy. Later, Iftekhar was rewarded with appointment of Adviser for Foreign Affairs by army government. Incidentally he was brother in law of Dr. Fakhruddin.

Role of India

Although UN and USA i.e. international community was in favour of democracy, India was supporting Moeen. There was a reason behind it. Acting High Commissioner of India S. Chakrabarti heard unexpected comments from Sheikh Hasina and reported to his government accordingly. Besides, Dr. Kamal Hossain and Dr. Muhammad Yunus went in favour of army rule. Later Dr. Gowher Rizvi was able to minimise the gap that was created as Pranab Mukherji was helping Hasina though Dr. Monmohon Sing and a powerful group of Indian government went against AL for obvious reason. However, as international community did not support that India also came on back foot. I was told that India agreed that they would not go against the rest of the world against popular support. Finally India told Moeen to make America agreeing to what he wants to do. Then Moeen decided to send his representative to USA with concrete proposal.

Dr. Yunus and Dr. Kamal went to New Delhi in favour of '1/11' era, which annoyed Sheikh Hasina, according to competent sources. There was a reason, why Indian authority went in favour of army rulers. India found the reason when Indian acting High Commissioner in Bangladesh S. Chakrabarti witnessed an incident related to a remark of a top Awami League leader. The remark was made against two leaders Suranjit Sengupta and Mukul Bose, incidentally who represent minority community as well, at the end of December 2006 in a reception in Dhaka. That 'objectionable' word affected a common community related to both Bangladesh and India. The reason why the remark was made is both reformist leaders went against their leader. Subsequently, at the same time, nine senior leaders of Awami League sent their complaints to Indian influential leader cum the then External Affairs Minister Pranab Mukherjee and to US embassy in Dhaka. However, the comment annoyed Indian authority which includes then Premier Dr. Monmohon Sing. Indian intelligence agency – Research and Analysis Wing-RAW has also taken it seriously. Accordingly, Indian government received a diplomatic note from acting Indian High Commissioner in Bangladesh.

Pranab Mukherji informed Sheikh Hasina that a blunder was made by the comment. AL President sent Dr. Gowher Rizvi as her special envoy to solve the created problem. When Moeen failed his mission eventually AL corrected the mistake done by its leader's comment. Moeen established authoritarianism which was a shift from what Bangladesh achieved since victory of democracy in 1991. India supported authoritarianism in Bangladesh since then.

Lt. General Moeen was given a red carpet reception by Indian government while he visited that country. General Officer Commanding-GOC of Rangpur area of Bangladesh Army Major General Syed Fatemi Ahmed Rumi, who was DG of Special Security Force-SSF during Khaleda Zia's tenure was the only general who accompanied army chief during the visit.

According to Indian authority, he was given protocol of head of the government. Indian government gave him six horses as gift. India knows how to do business with even military dictators. An example can be cited here in this regard that in October 1999 General Parvez Musharraf came to power in retaliation to his being sacked by then Premier of Pakistan Nawaz Sharif while he was on a flight coming back from Sri Lanka. In the changed world scenario, following the coup, Musharraf declared himself the 'Chief Executive' of Pakistan. However, then Prime Minister of India Atal Bihari Bajpayee congratulated him within very short time of his takeover. Bajpayee made a phone call to Musharraf and addressed 'Mr. President'. That was a signal given to Musharraf to proceed towards Presidency. Indeed, the general was in a dilemma on this. Eventually, an army person with uniform Parvez Musharraf declared himself the President of Pakistan.

Meanwhile, prior to '1/11' there was no High Commissioner of India posted to Bangladesh as Veena Sikri resigned from the position. Reason of her resignation was, she and 11 other senior Indian diplomats including her husband were superseded. A new High Commissioner Pinak Ranjan Chakravarty joined in January 2007. Deputy High Commissioner S. Chakravarti was discharging as acting HC during the period. Evidently, India played very proactive role in favour of a one sided election in Bangladesh in 2014. Indian High Commissioner Pankaj Saran did a shuttle diplomacy to USA and other western diplomats in Dhaka as well as UN envoys to allow holding election whatever it is. The country's argument was if this election is not held there would be a martial law. Veena Sikri, further argued, India backed the election for the sake of democracy (Daily Star 2014). This time the neighbouring country's fear is the possible military coup would be anti-Indian unlike the pro-Indian coup of 2007. Then it was said that, for the sake of continuity of constitutional rule the election would be held and within short time there will be another election accommodating boycotting political parties. Awami League leaders Tofail Ahmed (supported by another team member Ameer Hossain Amu in the negotiation with visiting UN envoy Oscar Farnandez Taranco, which was finally endorsed by the AL President Prime Minister Sheikh Hasina) and Indian side referred March 1988 and February 1996 elections in this regard and sought to allow AL to do same kind of election. On the eve of controversial 5 January election in Bangladesh, visiting Indian Foreign Secretary Sujata Sing's comment against BNP-Jamaat alliances, which was disclosed by the President of Jatiya Party Hussain Mohammad Ershad, has revealed Indian interest. That comment was undiplomatic as well. In the election in 153 seats of parliament candidates were elected uncontested means without election. Directorate General of Forces Intelligent – DGFI was given authority to hold election. Jatiya Party Chairman H M Ershad withdrawn his nomination within scheduled time, but he was declared elected. Likewise, many candidates either elected or their nominations were declared void. Ershad was arrested by the intelligence agency prior to election. Election was held at the direction was the government. Ershad demanded extension of filing of nominations, while Premier replied if I do so, BNP will join the process. Actually, election commission decided to declare 12 January the Election Day. Thinking if it needed to reschedule to accommodate opposition parties there should be at least a week in hand. DGFI people claimed, when government uses them they have to carry out their assignments without any choice. Regardless whether it is army government of Moeen or Hasina government of Awami League, DGFI does their assigned duty as per desire of the government of the day with high quality.

After the election was over, as the government was changed in India under the leadership of Narendra Modi, Indian High Commissioner shifted his position by saying that now his government's policy will be election is absolutely Bangladesh's internal affair and India would not intervene on it. That means that government can continue as it wishes for full term or so. Again that stance of the neighbouring country helps present government. Rather, Deputy High Commissioner of India Sandeep Chakravorty informed that without their help, Bangladesh could not win in recent two elections of Commonwealth Parliamentary Association-CPA and Inter Parliamentary Union-IPU. Additionally, BNP Chairperson Khaleda Zia expressed her intention to visit India to join the oath taking ceremony of newly elected Prime Minister Norendra Modi responding latter's invitation this year. However, the visit was not held, as Indian High Commissioner to Bangladesh sent a diplomatic note to his government that if it happens, that will give a wrong signal to politics of Bangladesh. Already opposition is in the better position. Finally, the 'Chanakya diplomacy' won.

Most recently former Indian High Commissioner to Bangladesh Veena Seekri made it clear that India's foreign policy and foreign relations are not changed with the changes of party in power. Another Ex-Indian High Commissioner Pinak Ranjan Chakravarty underscored the need for an accepted general election to be held in Bangladesh for democracy's sake. Veena's statement has been criticised by a cross section of people as she was comparing two top political leaders of Bangladesh and raised allegations against the host country in an 'undiplomatic manner', while Pinak's speech was appreciated instead. They visited Bangladesh in connection with a conference of former High Commissioners of both Bangladesh and India, which was held in Dhaka on 14 November 2014. Furthermore, due to maintaining extra-relations with her, a Pakistani High Commissioner was withdrawn from Dhaka at the end of Veena's tenure in Bangladesh.

It is obvious that India will do its own diplomacy. Similarly Bangladesh should pursue its own diplomacy, where the country can be benefitted. There should be a 'win win situation' in diplomacy. Since independence India has been taking its interest in Bangladesh, although previously it was not open. According to the diplomats, India is annoyed with BNP as its Chairperson dishonoured their President, who is the symbol of nation. Last year while President Pranab Mukherjee was visiting Bangladesh, there was a scheduled meeting with the then Leader of the Opposition Begum Khaleda Zia, which was cancelled by her. According to the Indian diplomats, former Prime Minister Khaleda Zia and her entourage visited India before Indian President's visit to Bangladesh when they were given high level reception, protocol and honour. But reciprocal relation was disturbed by the dishonour to Indian president. They opined, in the past India worked with military regimes of Bangladesh also. On the other hand, BNP says, on another occasion, Paranab Mukherjee did not meet once when he visited Bangladesh as a minister and some other ministers also followed this path. Then it was not taken seriously. On this issue, Indian point is the president is the symbol of nation and this position cannot be compared with ministerial portfolio.

Prior to early 2014 election in Bangladesh, India thought BNP and its alliances were going to form the government and due to this reason, they were doing business with BNP as well. Although AL is India's natural ally, regardless which party either BJP or Congress in power, India was doing everything covertly. However, they did something overtly following the 'undiplomatic attitude' from BNP, which was also not desirable, they agreed.

At the backdrop of India's extra-role in Bangladesh, US Ambassador Dan W. Mozena paid a visit to India prior to last most controversial parliamentary election held on 5 January 2014. American diplomat tried to understand India's mindset about Bangladesh.

Role of two Amins'

Brigadier General A T M Amin (known as Bihari Amin) worked for internationalisation of military rule of 2007-08. Initially he briefed US Ambassador, where his vindictiveness was exposed. He told Butenis that I was relieved and DG NSI Major General Rezzakul Haider Chowdhury was sacked. These were military's out of jurisdiction. He introduced me in my previous position intentionally. Brigadier Amin and a group of army officers went to Pakistan and Turkey to get ideas and collect documents to follow their model of governance including that of 'minus two formulae'. In Pakistan, General Parvez Musharraf ousted the then Prime Minister Nawaz Sharif and former Prime Minister Benazir Bhutto in 1999 from politics for ten years, which is popularly known as minus two formulae. Military backed government wanted to replicate this notion in Bangladesh during 2007-08 military rule. Subsequently, Ameen compromised with politicians on behalf of Moeen.

Military Secretary to the President Major General Aminul Karim played the most important role to allow Moeen to take over. When we were in a meeting of law and order on '1/11' presided over by the President Professor Dr. Iajuddin Ahmed at the Cabinet Room of Bangabhaban, Aminul dared to interrupt the meeting at one stage, saying that three chiefs are coming to meet the President and he also asked to make an end of the meeting. There was no schedule of any meeting of Chiefs of Army, Navy and Air Forces with the president that day. Moreover, it was just 'uncalled for'.

Journalist A B M Musa interviewed President Professor Dr. Iajuddin after '1/11'. The President said in the interview that MSP Aminul Karim helped Moeen and other army officers to takeover on '1/11. That was happened following his number of secret meetings with Moeen held at Bangabhaban and elsewhere. He opened the gate of Bangabhaban for them on '1/11'. All along it was he, who used to compel the President to rule the country during 2007-08. He ousted Minister Mokhles Chowdhury from the government and attempted to assassinate him a couple of times. Aminul Karim cancelled high level law and order meeting at Bangabhaban on '1/11' and a meeting of Advisory Council at 4 PM on that day. Aminul went to Sheikh Hasina after 29 October 2006 with army uniform violating the military rule. Moreover, when a political party AL chief Sheikh Hasina came to Bangabhaban, he told her, 'Apa, I was a batchmate of Jamal (Hasina's late second brother Sheikh Jamal who was also in the army)'. Previously, he lobbied for one of his brothers to gain BNP's MP nomination in a Chapai Nawabganj constituency in Bangladesh. He listed Harunur Rashid and Syed Asifa Ashrafi Papiya, both were contenders of his said BNP nomination aspirant brother. He also listed some government officials as corrupt in the trial list out of grudge.

According to a report of senior journalist Saleem Samad in 2008, Major General Aminul Karim was planted as MSP to Bangabhaban. Aminul attempted to assassinate me on 26 February 2007 in Dhaka through DGFI and on 7 September 2007 at a Janaza prayer of late Khatib of Baitul Muqarram National Masjid Maulana Ubaidul Haq at National Eidgah through uniformed army people. He made pressure on high officials of government to oust me from ministerial residence of Mintoo Road, where I was residing as Adviser to the President of Bangladesh and a minister. That very Aminul Karim was holding series of meetings with Moeen prior to military takeover on 11 January 2007. He, by convincing and with support from Moeen, managed to oust me from my government ministerial position illegitimately. Aminul Karim was rewarded by Moeen for his unprecedented supportive role, without which he could not takeover. Brigadier A T M Amin attempted to assassinate me. He gave me life threat on 15 September 2008 over the phone and lobbied to bring me back from London and after a couple of days a group of army officers attempted to kill me in London. A T M Amin was also rewarded as he continued unflinching support to army chief.

Bangladeshi former main opposition sets deadline to press for fresh election schedule

Rejecting the general elections on January 21 next year, **Bangladeshi** former main opposition Awami League-led 14-party combine demanded fresh schedule by December 2, otherwise, they will hold non-stop blockade from December 3.

At a crowded press conference here Monday, Awami League President Sheikh Hasina demanded recasting of the election commission by removing the controversial election commissioners, publication of flawless electoral roll and President Iajuddin Ahmed's resignation from the Chief Advisor's post of interim caretaker government.

She demanded appointment of a new Chief Advisor by the deadline for holding free and fair parliamentary elections.

Hasina also announced siege at the Election Commission Secretariat Tuesday, countrywide protest rally on Wednesday and sit-in strike in front of the Bangabhaban (President House) on Thursday.

"The election schedule was suddenly announced. The election commission is working at the dictation of a leader of a particular party (Ex-prime minister and former ruling BNP chairperson Khaleda Zia, " Hasina told reporters.

The Awami League president alleged that present caretaker government and the election commission do not want free and fair elections. Rather, they want to help rigging the elections in favour Khaleda Zia's alliance.

Former ruling 4-party alliance of ex-Prime Minister Khaleda Zia however welcomed the election schedule and accused her political opponents of disrupting the elections on various pretexts.

The Election Commission announced the schedule Monday fixing January 21 as polling day.

Rejection of the election schedule by Sheikh Hasina who ruled Bangladesh as Prime Minister from 1996-2001 would further deepen the political crisis in the country.

It may be pertinent to mention here, I worked in the UN system since long first as a diplomatic journalist cum editor and later in the capacity of a government actor. I had to seek assistance from the world body, while had been in the statecraft. It was required in order to continue with the democratic process and to stop ensuing probable military takeover. Before joining the government, I had to cover a number of UN events as a career journalist. I also attended the United Nations General Assembly-UNGA several years, including particularly the 1995 UNGA, which celebrated its golden jubilee. I did have contact with Kofi Annan while he was discharging the responsibility as the Under Secretary General. Kofi Annan could not have visited Bangladesh then as he was leaving the World body on completion of his two terms as the Secretary General. However, in response to my approach, he put emphasis to the situation of Bangladesh and sent his emissaries to Bangladesh in November 2006 -

Kofi Annan sends top aide to Bangladesh to help ensure peaceful polls

UN Secretary General Kofi Annan, concerned about current political developments in **Bangladesh**, is sending a top aide to the country Wednesday to help ensure peaceful and transparent general elections, private news agency UNB reported Tuesday.

Craig Jenness, director of the UN Electoral Assistance Division, will be in Bangladesh from Wednesday through Friday to meet with the Chief Advisor of the caretaker government Iajuddin Ahmed and other senior officials, election authorities, political party leaders and various interest groups, a UN official here was quoted as saying.

The official said Annan had been following the developments in Bangladesh with concern and wanted to offer UN support to the process "so that these important elections can enjoy the full confidence of the people of Bangladesh."

According to Constitution, a neutral caretaker government will organize the general election in Bangladesh within 90 days after taking office.

The former ruling BNP-led 4-party government led by former prime minister Khaleda Zia ended its tenure on October 27, and handed over the power to the caretaker government led by President Iajuddin Ahmed on October 29.

The former main opposition Awami League-led 14-party combine led by former prime minister Sheikh Hasina had staged three rounds of countrywide blockade since October 28, demanding for reconstitution of the Election Commission.

What diplomacy I started with Kofi Annan in November 2006, aiming to hold a participatory parliamentary election on 22 January 2007, later new Secretary General Ban-ki moon continued the mission since 1 January 2007. I and the visiting UN envoy Craig Jenness met one to one. For obvious reasons, the then UN Resident Coordinator Renata Lok Dessallien had to be outside during the meeting. There, I informed the envoy my observation that a military takeover is imminent led by Army Chief Lt. Gen. Moeen. I sought UN's support in order to halt planned military takeover for the sake of continuity of democratic process and for unhindered constitutional rule.

Moeen managed immediate past PM in favour of him to declare the State of Emergency on 28 October 2006 showing the 'Logi-Boitha' (Paddle-Stick) event. The dead bodies of that event were their capital what was result of army chief Moeen's instigation. He used DGFI to make it happen. Following the incident, there was dancing on the dead bodies. Whole incident was recorded by the intelligence agency. There was a plan to use this record to take over power. On the 29 December 2006, process of declaration of the State of Emergency was done at Prime Minister's Office – PMO. On that night power came to us as the President took oath of office of the Chief Adviser. The proposal of declaration of the State of Emergency was turned down by me. Later Moeen attempted two more times to take over power in disguise the same way. I foiled all these. This article will narrate more on this in the later part.

Consequently, an offer came to me from the army group loyal to its chief to be the President of the country. One of the reasons of that the President trusted me much and he was dependent on me. Moeen wrote in his book that I was most powerful in the Presidency. They propagated that I already became the de-facto President and Prime Minister. They really astonished, when I refused the proposal saying my agenda is to follow the constitution, to hold parliamentary election and to run the government which would be only routine affair. Virtually, the group showed seriousness, appreciated my role and asked for my new CV. Later they again failed to manage me when offered me the position of Chief Adviser. Eventually, the position was given to Dr. Fakhruddin Ahmed, who had also World Bank connection. Incidentally, previously Dr. Fakhruddin lobbied for the position of one of the Advisers' to us. Then it was not possible from our part to translate into action, as we had to consult with both arch rival political parties on such issues. The AL did not agree with the proposal as he was politically appointed Governor of the central Bank – Bangladesh Bank by immediate past BNP Government. Ironically, later same AL backed him when he became the Chief Adviser in military-backed government. When the military group failed to pursue me, they decided to oust me from the statecraft and use the President to serve their purpose. Actually that was their strategy to take power out from us gradually. Thus they ruled the country in 2007-08.

The aforementioned power monger coterie was against the judiciary as they were suffering from inferiority complex. At the part of that plan, Election Commission and some other institutions eventually out of the hands of judiciary. Military rulers first make civilians the presidents. Latest examples of that were Justice Abu Sadat Mohammad Sayem and Justice Abul Fazal Mohammad Ahsanuddin Chowdhury in Bangladesh and Justice Mohammad Rafiq Tarar in Pakistan. However, military-backed government of 2007 broke the precedence at the part of their plan. This way former Bangladesh Bank Governor became the head of the government.

The former Premier asked several times, why I obstructed State of Emergency again and again. Finally when it was declared on the 11 January 2007, she did not receive my call. In fact, she believed army officers much. In return, they betrayed her. Lt. Gen. Moeen, DG DGFI Maj. Gen. Mohammad Sadik Hasan Rumi, MSP Maj. Gen. Aminul Karim and DG SSF Syed Fatemi Ahmed Rumi were deadly against DG NSI Maj. Gen. Rezzakul Haider Chowdhury. On some occasions, they stopped DG NSI to enter President's room. I had to allow the DG to discharge his duty. Both the DGs of NSI and DGFI needed to submit their reports to the head of the government.

Although I failed to make the politicians understand, I was successful to make our development partners in this regard for the sake of Bangladesh's democracy. As I was worried for democracy, the UN and the USA has taken it seriously. Our common issues were democracy and constitutional rule. A number of army officers were against takeover. But they were unable to do anything against army chief. An army general raised a question in a meeting of the formation commanders about more media coverage of army people during the military-backed regime. He told that wrong signal was going to the people about army by this. In a week he was transferred to a less important posting of army. This way, Moeen gave signal to army officers. When General Masud went against Moeen's lust to capture power as the president, within very short time he was overthrown from army. When Moeen extended his service by one year, relevant file was processed without the knowledge of the second in command in army General Masud although then he was the PSO. According to the rule, the PSO was supposed to process such kind of file and to send to the President. Unfortunately and unusually, Brigadier Amin went with the file to Bangabhaban, where the President had no other choice other than signing it. In addition, two lady leaders were arrested at Moeen's desire. Other general's opinions on this were turned down. These are some evidences of Moeen's exercise of power during those days.

Moeen told Khaleda Zia that there should be election without AL. On the contrary, he informed Sheikh Hasina that she will be brought to power through election and if necessary without election. He instigated 'Logi-Boitha' and other blockade programmes. He also bluffed a number of people including General Ershad, B. Chowdhury, Dr. Kamal Hossain, Dr. Muhammad Yunus and Dr. Ferdous Koreshi. He floated a political party namely 'Jago Bangladesh'. Moeen wanted to hypnotise me as he did so to the former PM earlier. However, I could read him. For this reason, prior to appoint him army chief, I sent a 5 pages report to an important authority on this issue, where Moeen's plan and intention were mentioned. The report also briefed about other generals from whom army chief could have been appointed. Unfortunately, the advice was not taken into consideration. I called Moeen and his associates betrayers when they were in power.

It can be argued that If I did not halt the State of Emergency on 29 October 2006 night which was drafted and signed by the PM after working whole day at the PMO, it would have been declared. In November 2006 Moeen attempted to declare the State of Emergency on another occasion, which was again turned down by me. In third instance, after successful instigation by managing four advisers resignation from the government, army chief failed regarding this as we filled in vacancy and tackle the situation. When we deployed army countrywide in aid to civil power following CRPC's provision, Moeen included trial of terrorism and corruption in the terms and conditions of that deployment in line with his plan to grab power. Consequently, I managed to correct the order by the President in the greater interest of the country in order to hold planned parliamentary election. Finally, when the Martial Law was made inevitable by 12 January, with help from USA, I did my last job, and thus we halted the martial law. As both the rival parties supported Moeen's State of Emergency, one knowing and one without understanding, at last it took place. After taking over power, what was done by General Moeen that was visible in home and abroad. Yet, Moeen tells a lie. He was proud to be a green card holder of USA. It was proved once again that he was a coward army officer, when it was disclosed that he wanted to suicide after BDR mutiny occurred on 25/16 February 2009 (ManabZamin 2014).

<u>Moeen U Ahmed wanted to be president: Moudud</u>

According to a report of the Daily Star on 12 May 2013, BNP leader Moudud Ahmed said former Army Chief Moeen U Ahmed wanted to become president of the country. The report said, Moudud was addressing a book launching ceremony in the Supreme Court Bar Auditorium in the capital on the previous day.
"When I was taken to remand under army custody with my eyes blindfolded, I asked two young army officers what they wanted. They replied, they were working so that the army chief [Moeen U Ahmed] could be the country's president," Moudud said recalling his remand days during the past military backed caretaker government.
He was addressing a book launching ceremony in the Supreme Court Bar Auditorium in the capital. The University Press Limited has published the book titled "Amar Karagarer Dinguli: 2007-08" [my days in jail] by Moudud. In the book, he has also expressed his views about Prime Minister Sheikh Hasina and Opposition Leader Khaleda Zia who were also in sub-jails during the caretaker government. With former Dhaka University vice-chancellor Prof Emajuddin Ahmed in the chair, Prof Mahbubullah, and Prof Talukder Moniruzzaman also spoke.

The UN Resident Coordinator in Dhaka Renata Lok Dessallien's role was most controversial. Either she issued a statement supporting Moeen's takeover or Moeen blackmailed her making a fake copy in her name which he used in front of the President Professor Dr. Iajuddin Ahmed on the '1/11'. This statement helped army chief to convince army rank and file those who did not support Moeen's mission.

Below are some reports on UN special envoy's visit to Bangladesh:

UN special envoy asks Bangladeshi political parties to resolve differences
over elections

UN special envoy Craig Jenness termed the present situation
in **Bangladesh**worrying and asked political parties to resolve their
differences over the election through dialogue in a spirit of compromise.

"I am convinced that the principal political parties of Bangladesh, who have
themselves sacrificed for democracy in the past, will be able to make the
necessary compromise again," he told a press conference here Friday capping
his 3-day visit to Bangladesh.

"This concern and crisis need to be overcome in a spirit of compromise," he
said, wondering "Whether there is enough political will to reach compromise
through dialogue."

The envoy said, "If the current crisis continues, Bangladesh's international
reputation could be affected."

Asked whether the results would be acceptable to the international
community if all parties could not participate in the elections, Jenness said he
believes all political parties would participate in the elections.

However he noted it is important that the people should be given fair chance
to vote for parties of their choice.

The envoy said more works need to be done for holding free and credible
elections and the caretaker government, the election commission and the
political parties have great responsibility to create the environment for such
credible polls.

Asked if he has any formula to overcome the crisis, he said "I am not here as
a mediator but I am convinced that there are lot of rooms for cooperation in
resolving the issues through dialogue."

Asked if he thinks political parties are willing to sit for dialogue, the envoy
said he has encouraged the political parties he met during his stay to resolve
their differences through dialogue.

Jenness who was involved in many elections as Head of the UN Electoral
Assistance Division said a level playing field, a peaceful environment, a
trusted election commission, assurances of casting votes freely by electorate
and impartial voting and counting are critical to ensure public confidence in
any election.

He said UN is prepared to provide additional support to the electoral process in the country as Bangladesh is important to UN and plays a very important role in the UN peacekeeping operation.

Jenness said UN itself will not send election observers but coordinate international election observers from EU, Commonwealth, America would be sent to monitor the election.

United Nations Development Program (UNDP) country representative Reneta Lok Dessallien said approximately 320 foreign observers would be coming to Bangladesh to observe the elections.

The former ruling BNP-led 4-party government ended its tenure on Oct. 27 and handed over the power to a caretaker government headed by President Iajuddin Ahmed.

The former main opposition Awami League-led 14-party combine had launched three rounds of blockades since Oct. 28 demanding for reconstitution of Election Commission.

The 14-party combine will launch another round of blockade from Sunday if their demands are not met.

Source: Xinhua

UN concerned about free, fair polls in Bangladesh
Annan's special envoy meets Iajuddin, Hasina
Unb, Dhaka

UN secretary general's special envoy Craig Jenness has said the United Nations is concerned about free, fair and transparent general elections in Bangladesh and urged political leadership to resolve differences in the electoral process through dialogue.

"We're concerned about free, fair and transparent elections in Bangladesh and UN is ready to support the holding of free and fair elections," he told reporters after a meeting with Foreign Secretary Hemayetuddin at the foreign ministry yesterday.

Craig Jenness arrived here yesterday morning. Explaining the purpose of his visit to Dhaka, Jenness said Secretary General Kofi Annan has sent him to offer UN support to free and fair elections here and also express concern about some violent incidents that no one desires.

The visiting envoy said he would like to encourage the leaders of political parties to resolve their differences in the political process through dialogue.

In the afternoon, the UN envoy called on President/ Chief Adviser Iajuddin Ahmed at Bangabhaban.

The president told the envoy that all steps have been taken to hold free, fair, neutral and peaceful parliamentary elections and urged the United Nations to send observers to Bangladesh.

Listing the measures taken to remove hurdles to the polls, the president told the envoy that the chief election commissioner had gone on leave and two new election commissioners had been appointed to satisfy political parties' demands to create a congenial atmosphere for free and fair polls. He also told the envoy that the EC had announced the election schedule.

In addition, contract jobs at different levels have been cancelled and necessary reshuffles in the administration done for impartial elections, he said.

"The party who will secure electoral mandate will form the next government," the president told the envoy.

He thanked the UN secretary general for extending cooperation in advancing democratic process in Bangladesh.

In response, the special envoy said the UN does not like to see any political violence in Bangladesh and noted that all problems can be resolved through the holding of peaceful elections.

The envoy requested the chief adviser to take steps to establish peace in the country.

Jenness informed the president that he would convey the UN secretary general's concern about "political violence" during his meetings with the leaders of the major political parties.

Later, Jenness met Awami League President Sheikh Hasina and offered UN assistance to advance the democratic process in Bangladesh.

"I've come here as special envoy to support a free, fair and democratic election as the people of this country want a peaceful election," he told reporters after an hour-long meeting with the AL chief at Sudha Sadan.

Jenness hoped the issues, whatever they are, should be resolved through dialogue.

AL General Secretary Abdul Jalil, who was present at the meeting, told the reporters that UN wants free, fair and neutral elections and has offered its assistance if required.

Asked about the UN suggestion for political dialogue, he said the dialogue between parties is not required now as the matter is related to the caretaker government.

Jalil said the UN envoy expressed concern at the appointment of partisan election commissioners.

Awami League International Affairs Secretary Syed Abdul Hossain and former ambassador Ziauddin were also present.

Bangladesh to hold fair elections: president

Bangaldeshi President and Chief Advisor Professor Iajuddin Ahmed told a visiting UN special envoy in Dhaka on Wednesday that all steps are taken to hold free, fair, neutral and peaceful parliamentary elections, private news agency UNB reported.

Iajuddin urged the UN to send election observers to **Bangladesh**.

UN Secretary General Kofi Annan's special envoy, Craig Genness, arrived here Wednesday morning carrying his message for the caretaker government and the political leaders of Bangladesh that the world organization is concerned over the political situation stemming from electoral issues here.

He called on Ahmed in the afternoon in the first instance before talks with the political parties on both sides of the political division concerning the contentious electoral issues.

Listing to the measures taken to remove hurdles to the polls, Professor Ahmed told the envoy that the Chief Election Commissioner MA Aziz went on leave; two new Election Commissioners were appointed in view of some political parties' demand for creating congenial atmosphere for the elections while the EC announced the election schedule.

Besides, he said, contract jobs at different levels have been canceled and necessary reshuffles in the administration done for impartial elections.

The President pointed out that, as a constitutional body, the Election Commission has initiated all steps to hold free and fair elections. He assured the envoy of fair polls going to be held in the country, following such comprehensive groundwork.

"The party who will secure electoral mandate will form the next government," he told the UN emissary.

Reiterating country's commitment to the United Nations, the president said Bangladesh has been playing a lead role in various programs of the world body, including the UN peacekeeping mission.

He thanked the UN secretary general for extending cooperation in advancing democratic process in Bangladesh.

In response, the special envoy said the UN does not like to see any political violence in Bangladesh and noted that all problems can be resolved through the holding of peaceful elections.

"The United Nations is concerned at the violence on street," Genness was quoted by a President House spokesman as saying during the meeting with the President. He thanked the chief advisor for taking the initiatives for holding free and fair polls.

The envoy requested the chief advisor to take steps for establishment of peace in the country.

Genness informed the president that he would convey the UN Secretary General's concern about "political violence" during his meetings with the leaders of major political parties.

Both the President and the envoy observed with unanimity of views that all parties should come forward, realizing the reality, for maintaining peace and advancing democracy in the country.

Since the former ruling BNP-led 4-party alliance government led by former prime minister Khaleda Zia ended its tenure on Oct. 27, the former main opposition Awami League (AL)-led 14-party combine had staged three rounds of countrywide blockade demanding reconstitution of Election Commission paving way for fair elections due in January next.

Awami League announced Monday if their demands are not met, they will stage another round of blockade from Sunday.

During the blockades, there were dozens of people killed and thousands wounded in clashes between supporters of BNP and AL. The country's economy suffered a great loss.

According to the Constitution, a neutral caretaker government supervises the country's elections within 90 days since 1996.

Source: Xinhua

http://www.nytimes.com/reuters/world/international-bangladesh-politics.html
By REUTERS
November 4, 2006
Filed at 9:09 a.m. ET

As political situation in Bangladesh was rapidly changing, the readers may have noticed, media reports that the US Ambassador Patricia A. Butenis used to call me on exclusively during those days. In the meetings, we shared our common views, which were to protect and sustain our newborn democracy. I also went to 'Habib Villa' (US Ambassador's Dhaka Residence) to discuss with Butenis. Sometimes Deputy Chief of Mission Geeta Passi joined there. What we agreed is that we have to guard our interests, even with help from our friendly countries. Our international partners were pledge bound to extend their cooperation to our mission of democracy. We wanted to ensure democracy to be continued, which has been in the priority list of the UN, the EU, the Commonwealth and developed countries such as the USA, the UK, Australia, France, China and Japan. With reference to the Ambassador Butenis, one morning of those days, the Under Secretary of State Nicholas Burns telephoned me from Washington D.C. We discussed the prevailing Bangladeshi political situation on the phone. At the request of Nicholas, I arranged a discussion between Bangladesh and America on my mobile phone, where the President also joined later in the evening. Assistant Secretary of State of USA Richard A. Boucher spoke with us on the same occasion. That was a fruitful discussion indeed. Following this, as Richard expressed his interest to visit Bangladesh, which needed an invitation from the host country according to the diplomatic procedure, we responded positively in no time. Then acting Foreign Secretary and DG, America & Pacific were waiting at my office. I instructed them to send an official invitation on behalf of our government to Richard Boucher to make the visit.

Dr Muhammad Yunus stood by our government strongly. We accorded a reception in his honour at the Bangabhaban following the announcement of his receiving the Noble Peace Prize. Upon receiving the news, in no time I congratulated him on phone for receiving the prestigious award which earned honour for our country as well. Subsequently, Dr. Yunus asked the government of Iajuddin Ahmed to deal all destructive activities with a message to deliver a strong rule. He addressed the President at the reception of Bangabhaban, ''whole country is with you and please go ahead with strong rule. Please establish a strong government''.

Coming back to the issue of our parley with the UN and the US, accordingly, the visit of the US Assistant Secretary of State Richard Boucher has happened, where we worked out modalities that other than democracy nothing will be acceptable. Not only Boucher during his meeting with us on 11 November 2006 at Bangabhaban, Butenis also categorically commented that the demand of resignation of President from the position of Chief Adviser was impractical. Defying the USA and the UN's strong position in favour of us, Moeen and his accomplices betrayed that day blackmailing all concerned. They used a group of politicians, civil bureaucrats, civil society, professionals including media and businessmen.

The visiting Assistant Secretary of State of USA Richard Boucher categorically spoke on probable military intervention in Bangladesh that day. The Daily Star reports on 12 November 2007:

Military intervention won't help elections
Boucher says CG & EC must act neutrally
Diplomatic Correspondent

The United States yesterday said a military takeover would not help conduct a free and fair election in Bangladesh and urged the caretaker government and Election Commission (EC) to act neutrally to ensure each vote is counted and results are trusted.

"The situation here is difficult but the goal is [to hold] a free and fair election. I don't think a military takeover would contribute to that goal. That will be a bad thing to do," US Assistant Secretary of State for South and Central Asia Richard Boucher told a press conference at the American Club.

Boucher who arrived in the capital yesterday to assess the pre-election ground situation also called on the political leadership to lower the level of tension and violence and hold peaceful demonstrations so that voters get educated about elections.

"The voters need a fair choice. They need to make their decision through free and fair elections where each vote is counted and respected," he said.

Faced with a volley of questions on the chief election commissioner (CEC), he said he would not talk about any particular individual. As a whole, the EC has a very important role to play in ensuring the elections are acceptable, he added.

"Our view is…. a great responsibility lies with the Election Commission and they need to exercise that responsibility fairly but carefully in accordance with the constitution and avoid any outside influence so that people trust their decisions and election results," he said.

Richard Boucher, who will meet President and Chief Adviser Iajuddin Ahmed today, said the caretaker government must carry out its task in a neutral manner so that any of its decisions does not favour any particular political party.

There are a lot of issues to be settled by the caretaker government that needs more time to set up the groundwork for a free, fair, peaceful and credible election, he noted.

When asked about his meetings with BNP Chairperson Khaleda Zia and Awami League (AL) President Sheikh Hasina, he said both the leaders want free and fair elections and it would be better for them to reach a consensus on the issues respecting the constitutional process.

Asked how the election could be credible without participation of AL that seeks resignation of the CEC, the visiting US official said he hopes all political parties would participate in the polls and the EC should make sure that the people trust its decisions.

Boucher said both the political parties have a lot of experience in politics and they could easily settle many of the controversies.

He said the US would send observers to monitor the upcoming general election.

Terming the Dhaka-Washington relations excellent, he said his country would continue co-operating with Bangladesh, no matter what party gets elected to power in future.

He said despite Republican debacle in the midterm elections, the US government would carry on its efforts to strengthen democracy, healthcare and economic progress.

Above report is the proof of my successful diplomacy against Moeen's conspiracy. Mentionable, some newspapers including the Daily Star critically reported our activities during those days of Bangabhaban. Regarding US Ambassador's meeting with the President, it did not like or did not believe my briefing on the said meeting. In this circumstance, it approached the Ambassador, which I was informed that time. When Butenis supported my briefing and said I was the right authority and official spokesperson to brief the media. Then the newspaper reported with my quotations. One such instance is that the Daily Star reported then PM's Political Secretary was in favour of me. But reality was reverse. Harris Chowdhury was dead against me all along. He succeeded in conspiracy to stop my appointment in a diplomatic position. Later, he also lobbied against my appointment of Press Secretary first and then prior to my ministerial appointment of Adviser to the President, which he failed in both instances. In addition, Harris stopped the process of appointing former Chief Justice Mahmudul Amin Chowdhury for the position of the Chief Adviser of the Caretaker Government in 2006. A section of media was serving army chief and against me purposefully. They backed military led government later.

The said report of the Daily Star on my briefing on the President's meeting with the US Ambassador, can be seen below-

CA's resignation 'impractical'
Says US envoy
Staff Correspondent

US Ambassador Patricia A Butenis yesterday said some political
parties' demand for resignation of the president from the office of
chief adviser (CA) is 'impractical'.

Adviser to the President Mokhlesur Rahman Chowhdury in a news
conference disclosed Butenis' remark following a 30-minute
meeting between the president and the US envoy in Bangabhaban
yesterday where they discussed issues concerning the next election.

"The US ambassador told the president that the demand of some
political parties for resignation of President Iajuddin Ahmed from
the post of chief adviser is impractical," Mokhles told reporters.

"I have told them (the political parties) their demand is impractical,"
the president's adviser quoted the US envoy as telling the president.

Two issues featured prominently in the discussion — the
deployment of the armed forces in aid of the civil administration
and resignations of the four advisers, Mokhles said.

Later talking to the reporters, the US ambassador said she told the
president that the resignations of four advisers were 'unfortunate' as
they are honourable personalities and patriots.

She said the president agreed with her but told her that the four new
advisers are also firmly committed to working following the
footsteps of their predecessors.

About reconstitution of the Election Commission (EC), the
president told Butenis that if both the parties agree he would request
Election Commissioners SM Zakaria and Modabbir Hossain
Chowdhury to go on leave. The president believes the election
commissioners would agree to go on leave if both the parties reach a
consensus on the matter, Mokhles said.

Consulting with the two major political alliances, the council of
advisers headed by Iajuddin in last week finalised a package of
proposals including sending of Election Commissioners Zakaria and
Modabbir on leaves of absence and appointing new election
commissioners to reconstitute the EC. But the president in a sudden
move appeared opposed to the idea of sending Zakaria on a leave of
absence and unilaterally deployed the armed forces to maintain law
and order, prompting resignations of four advisers.

Following non-implementation of the package proposal, Awami League (AL)-led 14-party coalition, Liberal Democratic Party-led National Unity Front, some small political parties and different organisations of professionals have bolstered their demands for resignation of Iajuddin from the office of CA and appointment of a 'neutral person' to the post.

The president's adviser in an unusual move yesterday invited journalists in his office in Bangabhaban and briefed them about the discussion between the president and the US envoy.

The US ambassador discussed issues concerning the next month's parliamentary election and reiterated the US position of preferring holding of a non-violent, free, fair and credible election.

The president informed Butenis that the caretaker government has taken all necessary steps to hold a free, fair and neutral election in a peaceful environment and the US ambassador expressed her satisfaction over the measures initiated by the government so far, Mokhles said.

"The United States will continue supporting the caretaker government in holding a free and fair election for continuity of the constitutional and democratic process," Butenis was quoted by Mokhles as saying.

The president's adviser said Iajuddin and the US envoy agreed that political parties have come very close to solving the crisis and to overcoming their disagreements on electoral issues, leaving only some trivial matters unsettled.

They hoped that the parties would come forward to resolve the trivial disagreements through their wisdom, intelligence, farsightedness and sense of patriotism.

Butenis also apprised the president of her meetings with four-party alliance leader Khaleda Zia and 14-party coalition leader Sheikh Hasina.

On the army deployment, Butenis observed that it is necessary to ensure that the army acts neutrally. They will monitor whether the forces deployed in aid of the civil administration are working neutrally, she added.

President and CA Iajuddin Ahmed assured the US envoy that all the forces will discharge their duties neutrally during the election just like they did in the past. "I have already directed the administration

and all the forces to work neutrally," he was quoted by Mokhles as
saying.- Published on 14 December 2006.

["The people of Bangladesh deserve free, fair, non-violent and credible
elections", says US Under-Secretary Of State]
http://www.thedailystar.net/2006/11/30/d6113001033.htm
Daily Star, Dhaka, Bangladesh
Thursday, November 30, 2006
Nicholas Burns on Bangladesh
The United States has observed that the willingness of Bangladeshi
politicians to bury their differences of opinions is the key issue for the
country at present.
Speaking at the Asian Society dinner in Washington on Monday, US State
Department's Under-Secretary for Political Affairs Nicholas Burns also
noted that despite these concerns, Nobel Peace Prize winner Dr
Mohammad Yunus has earned an important distinction for Bangladesh.
"Can its (Bangladesh) leadership put aside their differences to lead the
country forward in peace? That is the central question to ask as we
approach 2007," Burns said. He also noted that there are reasons to be
concerned about the current state of political violence as the country
moves toward elections in January.
The under-secretary also urged the political parties to resolve their
differences through dialogue, as "The people of Bangladesh deserve free,
fair, non-violent and credible elections."
Burns, however, feels that in stark contrast to the political concerns, Dr
Yunus provides a positive vision for the country. "Bangladesh has recently
earned an important distinction, it's citizen Mohammed Yunus and the
Grameen Bank won the Nobel Peace Prize for their ground-breaking
efforts in micro-credit and other initiatives."
"He is a remarkably selfless person and he inspired me with his
ambitious and even audacious vision that all of the families in his
country should have access to capital to improve their lives," Burns said
adding he met with Dr Yunus in Washington last week to discuss how the
US can implement its own foreign assistance more effectively for
maximum impact.
Burns also stressed the pivotal importance of Bangladesh to the future of
South Asia because of its "Advantage of size, a growing economy, and a
talented population."
The US under-secretary, however, feels that Bangladesh must effectively
tackle corruption and failure to do so, will undermine confidence in
government and in the Bangladeshi economy. The US will work with civil
society and Bangladeshis to help combat corruption, he added.
The speech titled "US Policy in South Asia" was published in the US
Department of State website.

Top U.S. Official Set for Talks in Bangladesh
By REUTERS

Skip to next paragraph DHAKA (Reuters) – A top State Department official will visit Bangladesh shortly to assess the volatile political situation ahead of elections next January, the U.S. embassy said on Saturday.

Richard Boucher, assistant secretary of state for south and central Asia, was expected to meet President Iajuddin Ahmed, who is also the head of Bangladesh's interim government, an embassy spokesman said.

Boucher might also meet former Prime Minister Begum Khaleda Zia and her arch rival Sheikh Hasina, another ex-premier who heads the Awami League party.

Iajuddin took over as head of the caretaker authority last Sunday after Khaleda's five-year term ended.

At least 25 people were killed and hundreds injured in three days of violent protests over who should lead the three-month administration until the January polls.

Since then, Ambassador Patricia A. Butenis has shuttled between rival camps, meeting Hasina, Khaleda and leaders of the Jamaat-e-Islami party and the Jatiya Party led by former military ruler Hossain Mohammad Ershad.

Political analysts believe a visit by Boucher would boost efforts by Butenis to disengage the warring sides, at least for a week while Iajuddin tries to accommodate the demands of Hasina and her allies to make the voting free and fair.

These include the removal of Chief Election Commissioner M.A. Aziz and his deputies, whom the opposition accuse of bias toward Khaleda's Bangladesh Nationalist Party (BNP) and Jamaat.

The interim authority, comprising the president and 10 advisers, will run the country and oversee the elections.

Boucher visited Bangladesh in August and urged political leaders to cooperate to hold a free, fair and credible election.

On Saturday, thousands of supporters of Khaleda's BNP and Jamaat attended a noisy rally in Dhaka.

A two-member team from the Commonwealth Secretariat arrived in Dhaka on Saturday to conduct a pre-election assessment, officials said.

International moves on to end Bangladesh political deadlock

WEBINDIA123.com

Dhaka | November 30, 2006 2:20:59 PM IST
Alongside a number of local initiatives, international quarters have launched moves to forge a negotiation between the two major Bangladeshi political camps, sharply divided between Khaleda Zia's Bangladesh Nationalist Party and the Sheikh Hasina's Awami League, over the holding of the January general elections peacefully.

The deadlock, which was about to end with Chief Election Commissioner M A Aziz's decision to step aside last week in the face of a mass movement, intensified again on Monday when President Iajuddin Ahmed appointed two more controversial commissioners to the Election Commission, and the commission hastily announced the polls schedule with January 21 as the date for voting.

The Awami League-led political alliance has rejected the polls schedule and called upon the people to enforce another round of transport blockades across the country.

Concerned by the political turmoil, the United Nations sent an emissary to negotiate between the opposing parties, especially to pursue them for taking part in the general elections.

"I have come here to support free, fair and democratic elections as the people of this country want peaceful elections," the UN secretary general's special envoy, Craig Jenness who is now visiting Bangladesh, told reporters on Wednesday.

"All the major political parties should participate in the parliamentary polls and get equal scope for contest," Jenness, who met President Iajuddin Ahmed and AL chief Sheikh Hasina, said.

He underscored for holding dialogue to resolve issues, whatever they are.

The European Union, United States, United Kingdom, Canada, **Australia** and some Asian counties, including**China** and Japan, have also taken up simultaneous moves to bridge the division among the caretaker government, Election Commission and political camps to help to ensure credible elections.

The US Deputy Assistant Secretary for South and Central Asian Affairs, John Gastight Jr, is scheduled to arrive in Dhaka on December 3 on a two-day official visit to convey his government's stance for acceptable elections with the participation of all the major political parties in Bangladesh.

During his visit, he is expected to meet the chief adviser, advisers and top leaders of major political parties and civil society representatives.

The US Ambassador in Dhaka, Patricia A Butenis, on Wednesday night met with the immediate past prime minister, Khaleda Zia, to discuss Gastight's planned parley with Khaleda in the milieu of current political standoff.

It would be a 'follow-up' mission, within a month, in Bangladesh after the visit of the US assistant secretary of state, Richard Boucher, over the political **developments** in few months.

The British High Commissioner to Bangladesh, Anwar Choudhury, also held a meeting with Khaleda Zia, Tuesday evening presumably on issues concerning the parliamentary elections.

The Australian High Commissioner, Douglas Foskett, on Wednesday met President Iajuddin Ahmed at Bangabhaban, the presidential palace, where both of them observed that it is not important which party comes to power, rather the holding of fair elections was what mattered the most.

The UN resident coordinator, Renata Lok Dessalien, European Union ambassador Stefan Frowein, and envoys of the United States, United Kingdom, Canada, **Australia** and some Asian counties also held separate parleys with the chief adviser, advisers, Election Commission and the key political leaders apparently to help to resolve the current political impasse

Meanwhile, President Iajuddin Ahmed sent his adviser Mokhlesur Rahman Chowdhury to the Awami League president, Sheikh Hasina, and the BNP chairperson, Khaleda Zia, apparently to resolve the current political stalemate.Nobel Peace prize winner Muhammad Yunus has also urged the two major political camps to reach a 'peace accord' to avoid conflicts.

He suggested that even for forming a coalition government, political stability in Bangladesh was essential. (ANI)

http://news.webindia123.com/news/articles/asia/20061130/522746.html

On the morning of '1/11', I received the UN Secretary General Ban-ki moon's statement, which was handed over to the President. That asked to hold a participatory election and simultaneously to stop street violence. The message was literally issued for both the rival parties of the country with specific meaning. It can be understood by any lay man that the UN cannot invite military intervention in any member country. The European Union – EU's position was stronger against military takeover than political violence. Commonwealth's standing decision was to expel any country where Martial Law is declared. Latest examples of this were Fiji and Pakistan.

I had contact with the then Commonwealth Secretary General Don McKinnon, apart from UN Secretary General Kofi A. Annan. Following my contact, Commonwealth Secretary General McKinnon reiterated his organisation's position and warned any possible military intervention in Bangladesh in December 2006.

At the backdrop of turbulent political situation, a statement issued by the United Nations on 10 January 2007, where new Secretary General Ban Ki-moon urged all sides in Bangladesh crisis to 'refrain from violence'. A press report on this issue can be seen below-

Secretary-General Ban urges all sides in Bangladesh crisis to 'refrain from violence'

10 January 2007 –

Warning that the political crisis in Bangladesh has "severely jeopardized the legitimacy" of this month's planned elections, United Nations Secretary-General Ban Ki-moon today urged all sides to refrain from violence and seek compromise, adding he hopes the army will continue to play a neutral role.

*"The announced cancellation of numerous international observation missions is regrettable. The United Nations has had to suspend all technical support to the electoral process, including by closing its International Coordination Office for Election Observers in Dhaka," Mr. Ban's spokesperson said in a **statement** referring to the country's capital.*

"The United Nations is deeply concerned by the deteriorating situation in the country, and urges all parties to refrain from the use of violence. It is hoped that the army will continue to play a neutral role, and that those responsible for enforcing the law act with restraint and respect for human rights."

"The United Nations urges the non-party Caretaker Government and Election Commission to create a level playing field and ensure parties can have confidence in the electoral process."

"The United Nations is concerned that Bangladesh's democratic advances and international standing will be negatively affected if the current crisis continues. It urges all concerned to seek a compromise that will serve the interests of peace, democracy and the country's overall well-being."

The impoverished South Asian nation is slated to hold national elections on 22 January, but demonstrations and clashes between supporters of rival political groups since late October have left many people dead, according to media reports. A multi-party opposition alliance has also reportedly boycotted the polls.

The UN Secretary General's abovementioned statement can be accessed from the UN document below-

https://mail.google.com/mail/u/0/?ui=2&ik=4d7a4e1841&view=fimg&th=1487b371b5ebd9c1&atti d=0.2&disp=inline&realattid=f_i000qtad1&safe=1&attbid=ANGjdJ9pBuGW1EbX2zpFGqqD2rRm Hzo6dMkPlhvjW1QyF54ufSCGtC-EOtUATvrTnizSLL3N-vTJbBfjdWtUHYqe-02tKVrSkUd_jJ5u-1r0agTTZoCBJWCjABjzdr0&ats=1415121347526&rm=1487b371b5ebd9c1&zw&sz=w1256-h813

The way Moeen blackmailed the UN

Lt. Gen. Moeen wanted to establish that the UN asked Armed Forces of Bangladesh to intervene on 11 January 2007. His motto was to justify his coup in the name of stopping one sided election. My argument is, if that was a genuine reason, the question is why the UN could not stop the efforts of one sided election in Bangladesh in 2014. Why military did not pursue the State of Emergency again like 2007.

Prior to '1/11', Moeen U. Ahmed made a phone call to Jean-Marie Guehenno, an Under Secretary of the UN, who was in charge of 'Peace Keeping Mission', but he was not at his office at that time. Later Guehenno called Moeen back out of courtesy, which was blackmailed by latter, saying the UN asked him to takeover power. Actually, he wanted to make everybody fool. The reality was that other than the Secretary General, nobody was entitled to issue any statement on this highly political situation.

Like other military dictators, Moeen, a power hungry general, did spread rumour to all cantonments in the morning of '1/11' deliberately. Meanwhile, he served Brigadier Khaled Musharraf, a dictator for a short while in November 1975 after joining Bangladesh army in the same year. Then two groups of army arrested the then President Khandker Mushtaq Ahmed and the Army Chief Major General (later Lt. General) Ziaur Rahman respectively. Moeen was one of the army officers, who were in charge of the operation at Bangabhaban, confined the President (Shantir Swapne Somoyer Smriticharan 2008). According to him, since then he made his aim in life to become the President. When Khaled Musharraf's coup had failed after about four days, Moeen fled away from Bangabhaban, the Presidential Palace cum Office jumped through the wall from there and joined the mass procession comprising civilian and army on the street, which initiated a changeover on 7 November 1975. The two army officers have a similarity. For instance, Khaled Musharraf promoted himself as Major General on 3 November 1975 and Moeen U. Ahmed promoted himself following his coup in 2007. Another similarity is both coup failed to achieve their goal. In contrast, Moeen ruled the country for two years and could not have succeeded to become the President. It is said that since 1975 there has been a trend in the most of army officers that they wanted to be the President. Arguably, to become President is no wrong, but problem is using gun to occupy state power illegally. Looking back, since my early life my aim in life was to become the President of Bangladesh to serve the humanity, which was known to all those who were related to me. Based on the fact, first, I became the Press Secretary to the President switching over from journalism career when I was the President of Overseas Correspondents Association Bangladesh – OCAB. Eventually I was appointed the Adviser to the President and Minister in a very crucial regime.

Coming back to military takeover in 2007, on '1/11', Moeen also instigated army rank and file spreading rumour that he was going to be sacked and to be replaced by DG of NSI Major General Rezzakul Haider Chowdhury, which was totally baseless and false. Meanwhile, prior to Moeen's appointment as army chief in 2005, another Razzakul Haider, who was a senior general, was selected by the then Prime Minister Khaleda Zia. It may be noted that the NSI DG was a junior general. He was promoted from Brigadier General to Major General few months ago. He told, they wanted to make him an escape goat. Moeen propagated that the government created traffic jam in the capital city – Dhaka and also in wireless system so that he could not get the message through the cantonments. However, all these were concocted, fabricated and false. Notable, there were three groups in army. Major General Aminul Karim minimised gaps among them. He invited Moeen to enter Bangabhaban on '1/11'. In return, as indicated earlier, he managed a promotion to the rank of Lt.General later.

Excerpt is Renata's statement on 1/11:

MEDIA RELEASE

Attn: News Editor / Chief Reporter 11 January 2007

Press Statement by UN Resident Coordinator, Ms Renata Lok Dessallien, Dhaka

The United Nations is deeply concerned about the deteriorating political situation in Bangladesh. The national authorities have not yet succeeded in establishing conditions for Parliamentary Elections in which all parties feel they can contest freely, fairly and peacefully.

A strong statement of concern has just been issued by the UN Secretary-General Mr. Ban Ki-moon, the third such statement in the last three months.

An election in Bangladesh under current circumstances without the participation of major political parties would not be considered credible or legitimate.

The Armed Forces have recently been fully deployed in support of an election that some major political parties have decided to boycott.

The Armed Forces, including Police, play a major role in UN Peacekeeping Operations around the world, and are doing excellent job.

The United Nations appreciates the traditional role played by the Bangladesh Armed Forces in support of previous, fully contested elections through the maintenance of law and order, so citizens can exercise their right of franchise. However, should the 22 January Parliamentary Elections proceed without participation of all major political parties, deployment of the Armed Forces in support of the election process raises questions. This may have implications for Bangladesh's future role in UN Peacekeeping Operations.

United Nations Under-Secretary-Generals Mr. Ibrahim Gambari and Mr. Jean-Marie Guehenno of the Department of Political Affairs and the Department of Peacekeeping Operations respectively, will be contacting Bangladesh's Political, Caretaker Government and Military leaders tonight in this regard.

END…

For further information please contact: Mr. Sakil Faizullah, Communications Officer via email: **sakil.faizullah@undp.org** *phone: 8118600 ext*

2498, mobile: 01713 049900

GPO Box 224, Dhaka 1000, Bangladesh • Tel: (880 -2) 811 8600, Fax: (880 -2) 811 7811, E - mail: **rc.bd@undp.org**, *Internet:* **www.un-bd.org**

On the 12 January 2007 the Daily Star carried a report created by the news agency AFP, which supported the role played by Renata and blackmailed by Moeen. The report is as follows:

UN threatens Bangladesh's peacekeeping role
Afp, Dhaka

The United Nations yesterday threatened to strip the Bangladesh army of its prestigious and lucrative international 'blue helmet' peacekeeping duties if it mobilised to support disputed elections this month.

The warning came after the country's president declared a state of emergency and imposed a night curfew amid escalating tension ahead of polls, scheduled to take place on January 22.

"The United Nations appreciates the traditional role played by the Bangladesh armed forces in support of previous fully contested elections through the maintenance of law and order," said UN resident coordinator Renata Lok Dessallien in a statement.

"However, should the 22 January parliamentary elections proceed without participation of all major political parties, deployment of the armed forces in support of the election process raises questions. This may have implications for Bangladesh's future role in peacekeeping operations," she added.

The Awami League and its allies are boycotting the elections, demanding a total overhaul of the voter list and a swathe of other reforms.

It may be mentioned that before and after the '1/11' Moeen and Renata met a couple of times. They used to maintain excellent relations. Additionally, Renata did not deny Moeen's claim that the UN especially she as UN Resident Coordinator on behalf of the UN supported him. She also did not make clear about her abovementioned statement. When Moeen published his book 'Shantir Swapne Somoyer Smriticharan', Renata did not protest and refuse her involvement in '1/11' as army chief argued.

At last after three years, Renata refused her role in military takeover in 2007, which was played by in favour of Moeen when she was leaving Bangladesh completing her UN assignment. She addressed a press conference on 17 April 2010. Renata's latest statement was published in the newspapers on 18 April 2010 on the eve of her departure.

The Daily Star reported Renata Lok Dessallien's statement's about her role centring '1/11' of 2007. The news was published on 18 April 2010, which can be read below-

Sunday, April 18, 2010 Front Page

No letter from UN, no int'l interference

Outgoing resident coordinator Renata tells *The Daily Star* about post-emergency rumour in 2007

Rezaul Karim: International community did not interfere in any way and the UN did not send any letter that apparently led to the postponement of January 22, 2007 election and declaration of state of emergency, said outgoing UN Resident Coordinator Renata Lok Dessallien.

"International community including the UN did not interfere in Bangladesh's internal affairs…our only concern was to create a congenial atmosphere conducive to holding a free, fair and impartial election," she said in an interview with The Daily Star.

She categorically said the UN did not send any 'special letter' to the then Bangladesh government. "There was no interference. There was continuous urge for accommodation," she added.

Renata, who is going to take up her new assignment in China after more than a three-year eventful tenure in Bangladesh, did not agree with former Army Chief General Moeen U Ahmed's contention that Bangladesh Army personnel would have lost jobs in the UN peacekeeping mission if the army had played any role in the general election originally slated for January 22, 2007.

"This was never discussed," Renata added.

The former army chief in his book "Shantir Swapne" (Dream for Peace) said he received a phone call on January 11, 2007 from the UN Under Secretary General for Peacekeeping Guehenno who told him that the elections without participation of all political parties would not be acceptable.

"If the army plays any role in such elections, the UN will consider with due importance the withdrawal of Bangladeshi armies from the UN peacekeeping missions," Moeen quoted Guehenno as saying over the phone.

Renata said the UN secretary general expressed his concern over street violence on several occasions including those in October 2006 and early 2007.

She said several missions of the UN electoral specialists visited Bangladesh while the secretary general appointed a personal envoy who visited Dhaka in December 2006.

The envoy had meetings with major political parties and urged them repeatedly to hold dialogues, to be accommodative and to find a solution that both political alliances could accept.

"Telephone calls from high level UN officials to Dhaka were made to try to defuse the rising tensions so as to allow more space and time for the parties to negotiate an acceptable solution," Renata said.

The UN official said when the UN secretary general and any UN staff makes any statement, the copy is sent to the respective governments ahead of the issuance of such statements to the press according to international practice.

Asked about separate meetings of western diplomats with senior Awami League and BNP leaders at the residence of the Canadian high commissioner on January 11, 2007, Renata said the meeting with the BNP leaders was dispersed in the afternoon as the news of declaring the state of emergency had been circulated by that time.

She said the main message of all these statements and meetings were to resolve the issue through dialogue and in non-violent fashion.

When asked about the performance of the Fakhruddin Ahmed's Caretaker Government, Renata said, "we focused on elections but general criticisms were that the government was doing too much and it had broad agenda."

Renata recalled a number of impediments like two floods, cyclone, food crisis in the wake of price hike of food and oil in the international market and spread of avian flu. It is difficult for a caretaker government with 10 advisers to deal with all these problems, she continued.

Terming Bangladesh a complex country, she said, "Managing a complex country like Bangladesh, I think, is even more difficult. Each government faces challenges to implement its policies."

Asked about the performance of Awami League government Renata said the Bangladeshi people have to evaluate it. She said energy is a big challenge while population is increasing. Each year there is bigger crisis in energy sector, she said, adding that it will take time to resolve the problem.

Explaining UN's position on the trial of war criminals, she said the UN has received a request from Bangladesh government for information about how war crime tribunal operates in the context of other countries.

The UN has responded positively as we consider it important to share lessons of international experience with Bangladesh authorities in order to help them meet international standard, she said.

Renata, however, said the UN has not been asked for any other form of assistance in connection with Bangladesh's war crime trials, nor has it offered any additional assistance.

Asked about her farewell meetings with Prime Minister Sheikh Hasina and Leader of the Opposition Khaleda Zia, Renata said the energy and water shortages as well as other challenges like food security and disaster preparedness were discussed.

Renata stressed the need for strengthening democratic institutions to deepen democracy in Bangladesh and said since parliament is one of the most important institutions in any democracy all parties should sit in parliament and put their different agenda on the table for constructive debates.

She highly appreciated the formation of the parliamentary standing committees during the first session where chairs of the seven committees were given to other political parties. She also welcomed BNP's return to Jatiya Sangsad ending their long boycott.

Expressing her firm conviction that Bangladesh has a bright prospect, the UN official said the country has demonstrated its remarkable capacity to overcome crises — from the War of Independence to repeated floods and cyclones, to food security and many more areas.

"I do not minimise the very real and pressing problems that currently face the country.... all that's required is the strengthening of good governance. The key is already in the hands of decision makers. If their time and energy is spent in patronage pursuits serving special interest groups or individual interests, overall social progress will be sub-optional and beset with setbacks," she added.

As the Independent of Bangladesh reported on '1/11':

Dhaka, Friday 12 March 2010 / 28 Falgun 1416 / 25 Rabiul Awal 1431

Iajuddin was forced to promulgate emergency: Mukhles

STAFF REPORTER

A former adviser to the immediate past President Professor Dr Iazuddin yesterday said that taking advantage of the rivalry among the political parties General Moeen U Ahmed and some ambitious military officers had held president Dr Iazuddin hostage under gun point and forced him to install a puppet government through promulgation of state of emergency on January 11, 2007.

Mukhles, press adviser to the former president was in Bangabhaban on January 11, 2007 when top army officers met the president, said this while addressing a discussion meeting in London to mark the third anniversary of the 1/11.

"1/11 is a black scar on the history of the nation. It pushed the country 20 years back. The puppet government comprised some persons who had foreign citizenship and they did not hesitate to take steps harming the interest of the country. The architects of the 1/11 destroyed all the key institutions of the country, and in the name of anti-corruption drive they snatched away human rights of the people", he said adding that they forcefully realized thousands of cores of Taka from businessmen and siphoned the money abroad.

He also alleged that during the period between October 28 of 2006 to January 11 of 2007, General Moeen made attempts to promulgate state of emergency thrice but those were foiled. Mokhles said that General Moeen tried to promulgate Martial Law in the country by January 12, 2007 did not succeed.

"General Moeen forced the President to sign documents relating to promulgation of state of emergency arguing that there was provision in the constitution for emergency rule. General Moeen also ousted me from Bangabhaban without the permission of the President. I came under attack twice – on April 26 and on September 7 in 2007.

He alleged that the incident of 1/11 caused serious harm to the morale and professionalism of the army, which was used for serving personal interest.

http://www.theindependent-bd.com/details.php?nid=157523

Cancellation of Ershad's nomination

Foreign diplomats, based in Dhaka, did not take cancellation of H. M. Ershad's nomination in 2007 easy. They made a visit to his residence and expressed solidarity with him on that occasion. According to them, nothing is secret or hide and seek. They knew that former State Minister for Home Affairs Lutfuzzaman Babar was behind to disqualify Ershad through court in a short cut process. It was open secret to diplomats and conscious people. Earlier, Same Babar went to Ershad's house to bring latter back in the fold of 4 Party alliances. At the same time, Babar had connections with his political high command and with Army Chief Lt. General Moeen. He also maintained relations with western diplomats. Babar was playing vital role to split BNP and worked hard under Abdul Mannan Bhuyian. Later when that project failed and Moeen was asked to stop splitting political forces, hold elections and hand over power to the politicians, then Moeen's another strong hand Brigadier Amin led arresting Babar at a later stage.

It was evident that I have brought all political parties in the election by meeting their demands, although that was a very challenging job. But by cancelling Ershad's nomination, all efforts were made dysfunctional as agitating parties withdrew en masse their nomination on 3 January from the 22 January election, which paved the path to army chief and his group to declare the State of Emergency in Bangladesh in 2007.

European Union-EU was very vocal on political situation from October 2006 to January 2007. Canadian High Commissioner Barbara Richardson acted undiplomatically during the period. Australian High Commissioner Douglas Fosket was cooperative and time to time he along with Butenis appreciated my role. There was a group called 'Tuesday group' which comprises western diplomats based in Dhaka, who used to meet Tuesday. Time to time they made statements on Bangladesh political issues, which had adverse effect on the people. They thought the diplomats were cooking something or they were facilitating any move that was going on at that time.

At the initial stage, US Ambassador asked me to do something visible. When she saw that I was actively pursuing to solve the ongoing political impasses, having meeting with Sheikh Hasina and her representatives and also met almost all their demands then she was also serious in front of AL Chief. Consequently, Butenis understood the situation of Bangladesh well. She conveyed to AL Chief: 'if now you don't participate in election, something extra constitutional will happen and you will be held responsible'. Likewise, Allegations against Anwar Chowdhury were, 1). He talks much and 2). He lobbied Awami League high command for a probable candidate's nomination. Choudhury's position was on that due to the person being his relative. The person later became MP with AL ticket from one of the Sylhet constituencies on 29 December 2008 election. High Commissioner Chowdhury was also under surveillance by his own British Government.

Following my diplomacy with the UN and especially with the USA, all concerned agreed to help Bangladesh on the point of democracy. At my manoeuvre, two diplomats met army chief and Principal Staff Officer – PSO Major General Jahangir Alam Chowdhury on the 8 and 9 January 2007 and informed their common position that Martial Law will not be accepted, if there is a martial law all Bangladeshi peace keepers will be back home and in this case (if martial law is declared), there will be sanctions imposed on Bangladesh from the UN. That changed Moeen and his accomplices to go back to original option of the State of Emergency. When there was the move of the State of Emergency, I called Butenis. She replied on this issue that martial law has already been stopped. However, if it is the State of Emergency, Bangladesh Constitution allowed declaring it. We cannot help it. On this very day concerned top politician did not receive call of myself and other related leaders as I was asked to declare that earlier. As being opposing, was also questioned seriously that why I was doing so as the situation was very crucial. Contrarily, opposite camp was supporting the plan of declaration of the State of Emergency.

Later USA's support was sought to declare Martial Law

According to an exclusive report of the Weekly Budhbar, after taking over state power at gun point in violation of his oath, Army Chief Moeen sent Brigadier General Chowdhury Fazlul Bari to the State Department of USA with a proposal to allow him to declare a martial law (Amader Shomoy 2009: ManabZamin 2009). By which, he would be the President of the country, lift martial law and will release all detainees. Then, among two former PMs, anyone could be the Prime Minister while another one to be Leader of the Opposition. Upon receiving the proposal officially, the State Department officials stated: 'what the Presidential Adviser of Bangladesh M Mukhlesur Rahman Chowdhury predicted earlier about the martial law, this is what it is' (Bangladesh Worldwide 2013).

America followed its policy and asked the military authority to follow the Road Map to hold elections immediately and hand over power to the politicians. International diplomats had no other choices other than pursuing the Road Map to hold elections, when military intervention has already been occurred in disguise of the State of emergency. Initially a large number of people welcomed the changeover in January 2007 without knowing the mode of military takeover as they were fed up with political chaos and anarchy. On the ground, agitating political parties made the situation very serious and a military group was instigating to make the ground, ultimately which had been established as the pretext. Evidently, the USA responded very positively to my 'Save Our Soul' – SOS to save our democracy.

A Counter Coup was failed

During the visit of Lt. General Moeen U. Ahmed to Korea, a coup attempt was made in vain. Moeen made his visit short and came back home. Returning home he ousted Lt. General Masud Uddin Chowdhury and Brigadier General Chowdhury Fazlul Bari. First Masud was sent to the National

Defence College-NDC as the Commandant and within very short time the order was changed as he was transferred to Foreign Ministry. Subsequently General Masud was appointed Bangladesh High Commissioner to Australia. Brigadier Bari was made Defence Attaché to Bangladesh Embassy in USA. Eventually, Aminul Karim and A T M Amin betrayed them, which I forecasted. Meanwhile, after '1/11' Major General Masud was ousted from powerful '9 Division' of armed forces. It was termed by his colleagues that he was kicked upstairs. Indeed, then Major Gen. Masud was promoted to Lt. General, as he was appointed PSO in the army headquarters.

Although it was unlike, one of the major parties supported General Masud to oust Moeen. From the party high command, Major General Nizam and Major General Hakim were contacted to extend their support that move, which was against Moeen. But they did not agree on this as Moeen was powerful and they were loyal to him. A number of army officers were professional. Moeen used them and when his mission failed they were dumped to then Bangladesh Rifles – BDR (Presently Border Guard Bangladesh – BGB) and most of them were killed in a BDR mutiny occurred on 25/26 February 2009. According to the Prime Minister Sheikh Hasina, Moeen told for any operation against BDR, it needed two hours. Due to this, army operation into BDR Headquarters had not been happened at that time. In reality, army was standing by near Peelkhana (BDR Headquarter) and also was deployed at Dhanmandi Abahani Math, not very far from Peelkhana). It was argued that Moeen did not want any eyewitnesses of his military coup to remain. Consequently he became successful in this regard. Reportedly, Moeen managed some army officers' involvement with corruption, in order to check any threat from the army. Although, Moeen later argued that the PM was reluctant in taking any decision on BDR mutiny and she was in a happy mood having tea that time.

Regarding the issue of senior army officers' role, on two occasions, one Rashed connected me with Masud, while he underscored the need for making historic role by me for our beloved country. But he could not elaborate, as he was eager to discuss the issue face to face. Bari came to me at Bangabhaban in an evening and there was a proposal to manage Khaleda Zia, which I did not agree. I was told to run the country for two years. A thousand people were listed for the planned trial. I told ultimately two lady leaders will also be tried, which was Moeen's motto and thus he will take over power. Brigadier did not believe this. On the one hand, Bari was loyal to Khaleda Zia and on the other, Moeen was his boss in the army as well as he was loyal to Moeen. There was also a point, which was believed by army officers that Khaleda Zia may not come back to power through election, but Moeen will remain. Many officers in army thought Chief of Army Staff is the symbol of the armed forces. Officers always respect their Chief much in the army. Consequently, senior army officers those who were superseded by Moeen, did forget that previously Moeen served under their command. Many of them showed regards to Moeen when he managed army chief's position. I could not make Brigadier Wazed Thakur and Lt. Commander Saiful Islam Duke understands too that Moeen will take over, he wanted to be the President, will arrest both Khaleda Zia and Sheikh Hasina and attempt to arrange their trial. I told this to as many as concerned people involved in politics.

When I sent a letter of counter intelligence of DGFI, which supported my earlier prediction of military intervention, Khaleda Zia did not believe it. She told, she consulted with Brigadier Bari on this and was confirmed that the letter was baseless. Aminul Karim was desperate when I was consulting with Brigadier Wazed Thakur at my room on the letter issue. I also spoke with Bari on phone. Serious Aminul shamelessly entered my room and said this letter was nothing. He entered into that subject matter which I did not want to discuss with him. Aminul managed Bari and Thakur on this and connected with Army Chief. Moeen hypnotised khaleda Zia, her nephew cum PS Duke and other concerned officials that he was very loyal to BNP. All these, he was acting, they could not realise. In Bangladesh, the first military coup was carried out by Brigadier Khaled Musharraf on 3 November 1975, which was an abortive coup. It can be argued that 15 August 1975 changeover can be termed as first military coup. However, that was led by a civilian President, Khandker Mushtaq Ahmed, a senior leader of the then ruling party BAKSAL, which was originated into and re-emerged as Awami League again.

On the '1/11', I called US Ambassador Patricia A. Butenis and sought her cooperation to stop military intervention. She replied, at your request, the martial law was stopped and the State of Emergency is the part of the constitution of Bangladesh. The Ambassador also commented, both the lady leaders wanted the State of emergency, one thinks that she will be taken back to power and the one believed that this army takeover will make a change in the governance, which will help them eventually. Moeen failed to receive international support prior to so called '1/11' due to my shuttle diplomacy with a clear mission and vision in favour of democracy and constitutional rule. Later when he captured power by blackmailing all quarters including Khaleda Zia and Sheikh Hasina and above all the people of Bangladesh at large by creating a volatile situation with instigation to 'Logi-Boitha event and making our army deployment in aid to civil power dysfunctional, his written proposal was turned down by the US administration, which also established my empirical argument, analysis and prediction. Sometimes, some army officers openly attacked foreign diplomats with different languages saying we should not be dictated by them. Contrarily, that illegitimate military government surrendered to foreign power for legitimising and accepting Army Chief as President. Although western countries sometimes have their own agenda for particular countries for some reasons, they have some popular issues such as democracy and good governance, which made them strict on the issue of continuity of democratic rule instead of military rule. I was disclosing since Moeen was lobbying for the post of head of army. Others including Modud Ahmed has been supporting this notion after 'the patient had died before the doctor came' i.e. after completion of his surgery of democracy in Bangladesh.

Following Moeen's coup, after a reasonable period, I came to UK surviving a couple of attempt to assassinate me with instigation of Moeen and Aminul Karim where DGFI and PGR were used on 26 February 2007, 7 September 2007 and 26 April 2008. After staying a couple of days I went to USA, where I had to stay for three months. Then I worked with the US administration as well as with the UN system, which worked to stop Moeen from becoming the President again. At the same time, letter of Moeen was sent to the US administration to allow him to be the President by declaration of a short period Martial Law.

On '1/11' General Masud told me at my room, you are a veteran and we need your help. Then Brigadier Bari was accompanying him. Bari wanted to disclose the news of curfew for the night and informed this to Principal Information Officer – PIO from my office phone. Brigadier Amin started liaison with foreign diplomats. He informed the US Ambassador that I was relieved from the government position while cited my previous position, which can be compared that he forgot he was second lieutenant the other day.

Likewise, there was a political unrest during the tenure of previous Army Chief General M. A. Mubin, who replaced General Moeen U. Ahmed. Similar situation emerged afterwards especially in 2013 and 2014. During the time of present regime there were a number of chaotic events occurring in Bangladesh. Among them, there were Hefazat-e-Islam's events of 6 April 2013 and 5 May 2014, where a number of people were killed by police and Para-military forces. There were also chaos and anarchy situation during ongoing countrywide street movement until 29 December 2013. During this time the UN Secretary General's envoy Oscar Farnandez Taranco made an exclusive parley in later part of 2013. Following the world body's mission, the UN asked to stop one party election of 5 January 2014 in Bangladesh. Then the Bangladeshi relevant actors and machinery did not respond acting or reacting on the situation, as they were not ambitious like General Moeen, which can be argued empirically.

It should be understood by all concerned that to capture and to remain in power does not depend on foreign powers. Rather, the internal forces are more important here. Due to internal forces unflinching support Sheikh Hasina remains in power and opposition failed to oblige the Government to adhere to the democratic process of government. International support may be a bonus or supplementary in this regard. India was more strongly supporting newly independent Bangladesh, which emerged with their direct involvement, during staging a coup in 1975, but it did not intervene then. According to the diplomat Pinak Ranjan, India worked with military regimes of Bangladesh also in the past. All the countries should work with each other whatever government is in the counterpart's country.

Foreign support is one of the factors, which create a notion at least among the mass that they are with the government or not. Before appointing Moeen the Army Chief, I gave five pages report recommending the responsible authority to refrain in making him Army Chief. I mentioned the reasons for this. What I hypothesised then, by the time it has been proved by testing. After attempting all those activities, even now Moeen has been issuing false (lie) statements on what he did during two years military rule, which is unlike by other generals ever those who attempted coup either successful or abortive. When power came to me, the political authority did not allow me to sack him, as he was more than loyal. I told, Sheikh Hasina was openly threatening that Moeen and his accomplices will torture Tarique Rahman and Arafat Rahman, make an attack at their Dhaka Cantonment's Shaheed Mainul Road's residence and oust them from there. Meanwhile, the other side was as confidence as I had to listen 'if there is a coup, there will be a counter coup'. Ruling out probability of such action, I requested not to cancel General H M Ershad's nomination in a short cut way, which was not listened to. What I achieved by bringing all parties including the 'Grand Alliance' in the fold of election, that was destroyed by cancelling the abovementioned nomination.

Military takeover of 2007 was nothing, but an indigenous coup, which was absolutely born in the soil of Bangladesh, This notion was supported by the statement of Lt. General Moeen U. Ahmed, when he made it clear at a conference in 2007 at then Dhaka Sheraton Hotel that Bangladesh needs own brand of democracy. Major General Aminul Karim organised the seminar of so called own brand democracy at then Dhaka Sheraton Hotel. He was also advocating to form a National Security Council comprising three chiefs and other generals to control the government.

Analysing Bangladesh politics, it can be argued that those who are now looking for support of the USA and the European Union – EU even to an extent to India, they should depend on people of Bangladesh to govern the country. Bangladeshi people are the main factors to decide who will come to power or who will remain in power. Military rulers also spoke about own brand democracy. Hence, our politicians must follow the rule of game of politics. What will happen in future, that will also be decided in the soil of Bangladesh again. I predicted earlier that Moeen will attempt to be the President and if he fails to achieve so, he will hand over power to opposition camp of BNP following the theory of 'enemy's enemy is my best friend'. Present politics of Bangladesh followed the path of most Middle – East countries in case of 'after coming to power it is easy to remain beyond the tenure' (Zakaria 2010:220). Consequently, Bangladeshi democracy has been emerged as prime ministerial from, instead of parliamentary form of government (Chowdhury 2013). In fact, authoritarianism was established in Bangladesh. It can be argued that the country is heading toward a totalitarian regime or totalitarianism.

After withdrawal of nominations by a number of political parties on 3 January 2007, Election Commission had to follow the constitution to go ahead with scheduled election, which was stopped by Moeen with support from the present ruling party. Ironically, in the name of following constitution an election was arranged in 2014, where DGFI was used massively and political leaders were arrested. The election was held without the participation of major opposition parties when army intervention was not required like 2007. During our regime, there was proposal from H. M. Ershad to hold election keeping AL out of the fold. Even after withdrawal of their nominations, that election could have been better than what AL did on last 5 January 2014. As if, Caretaker government is necessary for AL to come back to power and after their coming back it is redundant. Similarly, constitutional obligation is applicable for AL, not for others to hold election without other parties if necessary. Evidence shows, the so called civil society, other than some exceptions, is silent on this.

Prior to planned 22 January 2007 election, following my meeting with Sheikh Hasina in the month of November 2006, a delegation of the AL called me on a couple of days exclusively at Hotel Sonargaon, Dhaka. It was led by Major General Tarique Siddique. There I followed up my meeting with the AL Chief and minimised gaps, which paved the path to solve the demands of rival political parties. I also met Khaleda Zia. Subsequently, I appraised the President Professor Dr. Iajuddin Ahmed on these meetings, consulted with the stakeholders including the Advisory Council, Election Commission and we had been able to met most of demands of the AL. As a result, the 'Grand Alliance' joined the election.

It can be argued, in comparison with 2006-2007 situations, there was a political unrest during the time of previous Army Chief General M. A. Mubin since 2010 as well. Comparing with previous regimes, political situation in 2013-14 was worse. During this time, a number of events were occurred. For example, there were incidents of killing happened at Hefazat-e-Islam's political programme on 6 April 2013 and 5 May 2014. Besides, ongoing countrywide demonstrations and street agitation movement had been continued until 29 December 2013. Following UN envoy Oscar Farnandez Taranco's exclusive diplomatic parley at the end of 2013, the government of Bangladesh was asked to stop one party election of 5 January 2014 by the UN. In fact, relevant actors and machinery of concerned country are held responsible to act or react responding political situation.

If actors are not ambitious they do not intervene in politics. It may be mentioned that General M. A. G Osmani did politics but after leaving uniform. Lt. General M Nooruddin Khan and General M. A.Mubin also did not take chances to takeover power.

To make it clear once again, it can be asserted that in 2006-07, I was alone in the government and statecraft against martial law as Moeen time and again wanted to declare it. When that was interrupted, as substitute, he wanted to declare the State of Emergency in disguise at least three times. He told the President that both the leaders supported him on this, while only Adviser to the President Mokhles Chowdhury was obstructing it.

Conclusion

It has been empirically seen that Army Chief Moeen U. Ahmed used governmental efforts to become the President of Bangladesh. He and his accomplices worked hard to receive support of foreign powers in this regard. However, he was foiled first by me as I did my diplomacy since long. Later he failed following submission of his official proposal to declare a Martial Law to become the President. I worked with the US administration as well as the UN system while staying three months in USA.

Looking back to analyses above, it has been also argued that India was in favour of Moeen for known reasons, but my diplomacy with the USA helped to stop our neighbouring country regarding this.

Whatever we need to do in politics, it is our duty to serve our country. Foreigners should not dictate our jobs. Sometimes, foreigners may have their own agenda. However, foreign power supports us in popular cause. They did not support military takeover in 2007. Ironically, general Moeen blackmailed United Nations on that occasion. UN Resident Coordinator Renata Lok Dessallien was responsible to support that military coup, which helped Moeen and his accomplices much to takeover. That was Moeen's only cover. Unfortunately, in this case Moeen used Bangladesh's participation in UN Peace Keeping Force as weapon. From that occurrence we need to learn lessons. It has been proved by this that the fear of losing participation in the UNPKF was nothing, but a tool to take over power. In conjunction with evidence, it has been proved that Lt. General Moeen's lust to power was the main reason, where other causes were secondary and tertiary. He used and blackmailed all concerned as and when necessary. Although I was alone in the government in halting martial law, the USA's help was one of the factors, which saved our democracy in 2007.

Bibliography

Ahmed, Moudud. (2013). *"Amar Karagarer Dinguli: 2007-08" [my days in jail]*. Dhaka: **The** University Press Limited. 11 May 2013.

Amar Desh, (2014). Joruri Obostha Noy, **Samorik Shashon Jari Korte Cheyechhilen General Moeen: Sakkhatkare Mokhlesur Rahman Chowdhury.**http://www.amardeshonline.com/pages/details/2014/11/28/261592

Budhbar/ManabZamin/Amader Shomoy/Thikana, (2009). Dhaka, Bangladesh 15 September 2009.

Chowdhury, M Mukhlesur Rahman. (2014). *USA's Efforts For A New Election To Restore Democracy In Bangladesh.* Countercurrents.org 15 February 2014

Chowdhury, M Mukhlesur Rahman. (2014). *Good Governance In Bangladesh: A Quest For Democracy.* Countercurrents.org 19 January, 2014

Chowdhury, M Mukhlesur Rahman. (2014). *Why The Military Intervened In Bangladesh Politics?* Countercurrents.org 10 January, 2014

Chowdhury, M Mukhlesur Rahman. (2013). *Political Deadlock: Will History Repeat Itself In Bangladesh?* Countercurrents.org 30 December, 2013

Chowdhury, M Mukhlesur Rahman, (2010). *Iajuddin was forced to promulgate emergency: Mukhles* the Independent,Dhaka Friday 12 March 2010

Daily Star, (2014). *'It was essential and necessary to hold the general elections'* 25 November 2014 found at **http://www.thedailystar.net/it-was-essential-and-necessary-to-hold-the-general-elections-51877**

Daily Star, (2006). *UN concerned about free, fair polls in Bangladesh Annan's special envoy meets Iajuddin, Hasina.* Unb, Dhaka 30 November 2006 found at **http://archive.thedailystar.net/2006/11/30/d6113001044.htm**

Daily Star, (2006). *Military intervention won't help elections Boucher says CG & EC must act neutrally* 12 November 2006 found at**http://archive.thedailystar.net/2006/11/12/d6111201033.htm**

Daily Star (2006). *CA's resignation 'impractical' Says US envoy* 14 December 2006. Available at**http://archive.thedailystar.net/2006/12/14/d61214012615.htm**

Daily Star, (2006)   Nicholas Burns on Bangladesh. 30 November 2006 available at**http://www.thedailystar.net/2006/11/30/d6113001033.htm**

Ittefaq, (2014). *Samorik Shashon Jari Korte Cheyechhilen General Moeen Rastroptio Sabek Upodeshta Mokhlesur Rahmaner Sakkhatkar.* **30 November 2014 Found** at **http://www.ittefaq.com.bd/print-edition/first-page/2014/11/30/17702.html**

Ittefaq, (2006). Ittefaq, (2006). *'Obadh O Shantipurno Nirbachon Onushthane Sobrokom Podokkhep Neaya Hoyecche – Jatisongho Bishesh Dutke Rashtropoti'* http://www.ittefaq.com.bd/print-edition/first-page/2014/11/30/17702.html

Manabzamin, (2014). *Moeen wanted to suicide.* 18 November 2014

United Nations (2007).   Secretary-General Ban urges all sides in Bangladesh crisis to 'refrain from violence' 10 January 2007 available at**https://mail.google.com/mail/u/0/?ui=2&ik=4d7a4e1841&view=fimg&th=1487b371b5ebd9c1&attid=0.2&disp=inline&realattid=f_i000qtad1&safe=1&attbid=ANGjdJ9pBuGW1EbX2zpFGqqD2rRmHzo6dMkPlhvjW1QyF54ufSCGtC-EOtUATvrTnizSLL3N-vTJbBfjdWtUHYqe-02tKVrSkUd_jJ5u-1r0aqTTZoCBJWCjABjzdr0&ats=1415121347526&rm=1487b371b5ebd9c1&zw&sz=w1256-h813**

WEBINDIA123.com, (2006). *International moves on to end Bangladesh political deadlock.* 30 November 2006 found at**http://news.webindia123.com/news/articles/asia/20061130/522746.html**

Xinhua, (2006). *Bangladeshi former main opposition sets deadline to press for fresh election schedule.* **28 November 2006 access to available** at**http://english.people.com.cn/200611/28/eng20061128_325742.html**

Xinhua, (2006). *Kofi Annan sends top aide to Bangladesh to help ensure peaceful polls* **28 November 2006 available at**

http://english.people.com.cn/200611/28/eng20061128_326086.html

Xinhua, (2006).*UN special envoy asks Bangladeshi political parties to resolve differences over elections.* 1 December 2006 **available** at**http://english.people.com.cn/200612/01/eng20061201_327356.html**

Xinhua, (2006).*Bangladesh to hold fair elections: president*   29 November 2006**available at http://english.people.com.cn/200611/29/eng20061129_326560.html**

Zakaria, F. (2010). *Islam, Democracy, and Constitutional Liberalism,* Essential Readings in Comparative Politics, W.W. North & Company New York. London

Chapter 2

Why The Military Intervened In Bangladesh Politics?

By M Mukhlesur Rahman Chowdhury

10 January, 2014

An innovative system of Caretaker Government was abolished following 2007 military intervention which created a political crisis prolonged until present prevailing stalemate in Bangladesh.

'Why the military has intervened in Bangladesh politics' needs to be answered. Unfortunately few research works have adequately examined the causes of and conditions for military intervention. The scholarly studies of Emajuddin Ahamed, Zillur Rahman Khan, and Hassan Uzzaman are worth mentioning on this as far as existing literature are concerned. Experts on Bangladesh politics Talukdar Maniruzzaman, Rounaq Jahan, and Marcus Franda have dealt with the military intervention issue on different occasions as well. About two army coups occurred in 1975, Lawrence Lifschultz and Anthony Mascaranhas addressed in their books in detail.

According to literature, mainly two reasons were identified for military intervention. They are: military factors and political elements. To find out the causes and conditions for the military intervention it needs to identify certain elements involved within. The major elements are corporate interests of military, conspiracy against the regime, personal motives of coup makers, political issues in the corporatist interpretation, divisions in political parties, lack of political institutionalisation or the failure of civilian regimes.

Some scholars argued that the developing nations have been suffering from political problems, which caused 'bad governance'. The problems include political chaos and anarchy; broaden corruption, absence of rule of law, transparency as well as accountability (Udogu, 2000). Since 1991 Bangladesh is evidence of all indicators (Hagerty, 2007).

Ball (1981) analytically evaluates the developing countries militaries political role for two reasons. First, the military-backed governments are least responsive to the needs and voices of the poor majority. Besides, military-dominated governments use arms far more frequently than civilian-dominated governments in order to curb civilian demands and unrest. Second, with the increasing role of the military in politics, its control over scarce resources of the country increases as well. For this reason, a greater amount of these scarce resources has been channelled into the military sector or activities closely related to the military.

Ball identifies four major beneficiaries' societal groups that most likely benefit from the involvement of the military in the economic and political life of a country: domestic civilian groups, the military as an institution, and the individuals within the military and foreign groups. Corruption is an important element attached to military intervention in political and the economic life of the country. It has been seen that when the army seek to get involved in the political process of a country, allies are sought among bureaucrats, technocrats and politicians.

'In military-dominated government the collaboration of the civil service is vital because a country cannot be administrated solely with military man power, not even one as entrenched as that in Brazil, Thailand and Indonesia. It is generally argued that the military and the civilian bureaucracy are best allies' (Edward Feit, 1973).

Apart from the above research works Samuel Huntington, Morris Janowitz, Syed Sirajul Islam, Hamza Alavi, Ahmed, Rahman, Chowdhury, Badaruddin Umar, Borhanuddin Khan Jahangir, Alan Lindquist, Peter Bertocci, William Sloan, Khan, among others, analysed in their books and journals on military intervention, politics and governance of Bangladesh where failure of politicians, corruption and military leaders lust of power came as cause of military intervention.

On the research issue, Bangladesh has been neglected as many researchers think there are similarities with Pakistan although there are dissimilarities too and dimension is also different as Bangladesh has no ethnic, religious or sectarian problem whereas Bangladeshi is mostly a homogeneous nation. There is a problem to pursue this kind of research by Bangladeshi researchers is fear of persecution by military. Still Directorate General of Forces Intelligent (DGFI) is playing key role in running the government under civilian cover. An editor is now in jail and another journalist left the country as could came out of prison and there are many those who were abducted. Human rights situation is bad there although in economic field Bangladesh is doing well when even recession is going on in developed countries. Another reason of reluctance in doing research is many people think external powers are involved in military intervention. Due to rampant corruption in Bangladesh politics a vast majority of the people dislike politics and sometimes do not feel bad as did earlier on military intervention. It is better to study on Bangladesh politics from outside the country. These days academics are becoming more interested about it. Those who are pursuing PhD on related topics about Bangladesh most of their research works are superficial and sometimes far from truth as they are not in a position to dig out the truth. I witnessed many untold facts while was in the helm of affairs of the country which are being researched in other way round. My track record of integrity as well as being courageous will be able to find problems and solutions into it, which will discover ways for the actors and development partners to build a better country and help researches to gain the right issues in right place.

'Why the explanations of military intervention in politics of Bangladesh are not adequate':

As far as military intervention is concerned, the few scholarly studies have adequately examined its root causes. As there are lacking in understanding Bangladesh politics correctly, the superficial research works have been continuing in most of the cases. It was found that there are two factors involved in military intervention in politics. They are Corporatist and structuralist. One argument is military factors are the main elements here while the other scholars group argues that it is the political elements. The argument in favour of political factors seems to be weak. Only a few authors undertake the structuralist approach. They treat military intervention as a peripheral theme. In corporatist strand, all agree that there is no single factor in military intervention. The distinct characteristic of this study is practicality of the situation what gives blame on politicians. The authors of this group try to connect military with politicians giving the first party upper hand. Emajuddin Ahamed represents this group and recognises that in the political vacuum (systemic weaknesses) army takes over. His explanations are not adequate as only emphasised on one side of the coin.

By reviewing it can say that Ahamed fails to make a direct connection between the 'systemic weakness' and military intervention. His study could not answer why such weakness arises and why military needs to seize state power. Hassan Uzzaman, Peter Bertocci, Ahamed, Khan, Jahan, Franda, Maniruzzaman and Lifschultz rely more or less on the hypothesis that coups were occurred on same issues e.g. failure of politicians, military interests and corruptions. They interpret the political situations of Bangladesh in the light of the late 1950s-1970s military intervention theories when there was a different situation as bipolar world was in existence. Among two super powers America and the then Soviet Union were in rivalry position on military intervention issue and one used to use veto power against another in the United Nations. On the other hand, because of changed political scenario with the unipolar world there are risks of losing participation in the UN Peace Keeping Forces at present military intervention faces obstacles. Now-a-days in the changed political situation, army commands instigate rival political forces for their own interest and at the same time showed government, people and external factors that they are unwilling to take over, they do it once they are bound to do so when country is at stake as people want get rid of political chaos and anarchy and do welcome military intervention. However, at the same time highest degree of rivalry in political parties helps some highly ambitious people in the top of armed forces for military intervention for their own interest. These developments in politics are yet to address in various research works, which is definitely inadequate for the scholarly studies in this field.

The literature on military intervention first emphasises the unique characteristics of the military establishment, which is considered to be the prime cause of actions of military. Study in this field has been continuing with the developments of military rule in different countries. Although authors like Samuel Huntington thought that military explanations are not sufficient to explain the reasons of military coups. Besides, there is a strong tendency in the literature to overemphasis the organisational aspect of the military.

Ahamed and Khan evaluate Bangladesh army's colonial legacy and 'apolitical' role while have been claiming that this army functions as the guardian of society. According to Ali Riaz, the most serious flaw in this type of interpretation is drawing the bottom-line that the military is an apolitical organisation while involving beyond their constitutional role. Moreover, this way of argument ignores the fact that the military is an organ of the state. Both Ahamed and Khan inherited these weaknesses from the general line of arguments put forth in the works of Pauker, Pye, Janowitz and Feit. According to them the military organisation can be treated as an independent variable.

Both Ahamed and Khan agree with Finer, Nordlinger, Dowse and Gutterdige about corporate interests as one of the main factors in military intervention in politics as they considered some case studies of military intervention in different countries during pre and post last two world wars. But it is agreed by other studies that coups cannot be attributed to corporate interests alone. Ahamed rely on two other factors other than corporate interests of army, which are the formation of 'Jatiya Rakhhi Bahini' (National Security Force) and creation of division in army as 'freedom fighters' and 'repatriated'. Khan's opinion is same on this. However, following 1975 coups Bangladesh faced more military interventions, both successful and abortive. In this case, it cannot say that these are only factors or causes to legitimise military intervention.

The main hypothesis of Baladas Ghosal's latest article 'The Anatomy of Military Interventions in Asia: The Case of Bangladesh' is that a new pattern of military involvement in politics is emerging in countries such as Pakistan and Bangladesh, which will call 'power without responsibility and accountability'. The article referred 2007 coup as saying, 'the military intervention has both long- and short-term implications for political developments in Third World countries and, thus, requires closer scrutiny and analysis'. The weakness of this research is it could not assess the causes and conditions availing in the country prior to military intervention happened in 2007.

Regarding failure of the military backed government of 2007-08, Maryam Mastoor argues that the lack of public participation and unlawful in its existence as well as unconstitutional status led to its drastic failure made it more vulnerable. But it did not mention about the military government's huge corruption and torture on politicians and people out of grudge.

According to recent findings of a paper of Florida State University titled 'What Accounts for Military Interventions in Politics: A Cross- National Comparison', it supports socio-economic and political institutionalisation as having the most significant impact on the incidence of coups. It emphasises more on African and Latin American military interventions while could not address real problems of Asian especially Bangladesh context of indigenous style political crises which include dynamism of politics of discord, enmity and mistrust.

Referring 1975 coup, Franda and Maniruzzaman mention that personal motives of coup makers are important factors. Although 2007 military intervention was dependent on army chief's lust to be the President of the country, according to all major stakeholders including two major political parties and local and international newspapers. Lieuwen, Finer and Decalo argues that apart from other factors including political problems, corporate interests, corruption most common issue is individual self-interest which causes military intervention. Followed by 1975 coup there were more coups took place in Bangladesh. These examples are clear indication here that the personal motives theory is not adequate to discover the actual cause of military interventionism in Bangladesh.

As Lifschultz points out the issue of conspiracy against the regime with external involvement, it can be said that the organisational aspect of the military cannot be ignored. It has been seen that military has a monopoly over the means of coercion.

Ahamed, Jahan and Bertocci analyse that failure of politicians or civilian government is one of the principal causes of military intervention. Corruption and economic crisis are discussed here as well. They referred 1975 and 1982 coups in this regard. Military rulers raise this issue in after all interventions. The claim of corruption and inefficiency may be among the causes as all military rulers allege, but these are the only reason is questionable. Before coming to conclusion on this research one should point to the sources of the crisis: class composition of the ruling elites, nature/position of the state in the global economic system. Position of Bangladesh Army and situation of Bangladesh are quite different and unique as deviation from promise and agreements are there. Mutual trust is absent in politics among stakeholders are very visible. It needs to understand complexity of indigenous and different type of Bangladeshi characteristics which was formed and developed with colonial legacy, war of secession and democratic movements.

Without understanding the context and reality of Bangladesh politics it cannot be drawn outline of research to restructure and reform of governance. Regarding Bangladesh Army, it was established through a war. The armed forces think they are part of it unlike other armies and their sense of belonging is different from other disciplined armies.

Moudud Ahmed in his book 'Democracy and the Challenge of Development – A Study of Politics and Military Interventions in Bangladesh' mentions about the crisis' (UPL 1995) The power of governing the state moved from the hands of the politicians to the combined class of officers and technocrats – which changed the character and complexion of the administration as a whole'. However he did not cite any reference of corruption of 1982-90 military regimes where he played as an actor.

It seems, as studying, that there are both strengths and weaknesses in the existing literature of military intervention. In most of the cases, research works are undertaken depending on only general aspects of military intervention. Furthermore, sometimes the research is done superficially. This review shows that some relevant and important issues have not been really taken into consideration while pursuing the scholarly studies. Thus, it can be said that the explanations of military intervention in politics of Bangladesh are not adequate.

The theory of Historical Institutionalism

The theory of Historical Institutionalism (HI) was not previously examined in Bangladesh politics with its full potential. Historical Institutionalism (HI) provides a valid and powerful theory to evaluate the democratic development as well as legacies. The central concept of HI is that historic policy choices of institutions impact on future policy. The policy is based on long-range determining effect. Here history matters as 'path dependency'. Behind the HI approach Steinmo, Thelen and Longstreth (1991) contributed main role. In path dependency past decisions set the context in which contemporary decisions are taken.

The important things for my research project which are to deal with largely with political and cultural institutional factors such as the constitution, distrust and role of the military. Historical institutionalism analysis is useful to analyse Bangladesh politics because of the factors that are clearly subject to path dependency. It is appropriate because these institutions and hindering factors have evolved over time based on complex interacting factors. This is exactly the type of analysis that historical institutionalism was designed for. Bangladesh inherited historical legacy that affects politics and thereby international relations. It has critical juncture as well. For these reasons HI is distinct and most productive approach as theory here.

For example, people's rights deprivations in Bangladesh, although begun under colonial era, have shown a high degree of 'path dependent' continuity beyond independence and into the present day. The lack of significant reform is partly due to the incumbent interest groups, namely the ruling party politicians, a section of civil-military bureaucrats close to government's hierarchy, and particular commercial and private interests, which have continued to benefit, despite the creation of mass supporter of democracy and good governance.

Good governance

There are both positive and negative sides of 'good' governance and that is why I put good under inverted comma. Regarding institutional reform and strengthening of Anti-Corruption Commission are World Bank's agendas although there are criticism which includes imperialism and extension of capitalism. Besides, there should be combination of Bangladeshi indigenous model of democracy with donor agencies popular 'good governance' theory. Good governance has connection with the World Bank prescription and in some cases to disburse aid is conditional. Recently WB withdrew an approved fund worth $3 billion for the construction of the long awaited 'Padma Multi-purpose Bridge' due to alleged involvement of government corruption for what a minister had to resign. Although this was an intervention yet it is acceptable for the sake of sustainable democracy (Daily Star 2012, World Bank 2013). Although Bangladesh opted for Westminster type of democracy, the country has been witnessing 'all powerful Prime Ministerial form of government' which replaced earlier Presidential system of government (Daily Star 2011). To get rid of governance problem Bangladesh needs major structural reform in government sector (UNDP 2012) for its sustainable development and survival of its democracy (Chowdhury 2008).

There are disputes and debates on the theories as well as on the prospects of 'good governance'.

The strengths of the notion of 'good governance':

It is supportive and cooperative relationships between government, civil society and the private sector. It is combination of some elements such as participation, accountability, transparency of decision-making, the rule of law and predictability. Moreover, sometimes civil liberties, democratic practices, and access to information are included to the list. As far as the developing countries are concerned, donor assistance to strengthen governance has focused on empowerment and capacity-building.

According to the World Bank, UNDP, OSCE, USAID, and other donor agencies, good governance consists of political and economic dimensions. The political dimension is divided into four parts: government legitimacy; government accountability; government competence; and human rights or rule of law. On the other hand, the economic dimension has four components: public sector management; organisational accountability; rule of law including contracts, property rights; and transparency includes freedom of information.

The weaknesses of the notion of 'good governance':

The frameworks are normative in character.

Dr. Mark Orkin suggests two main reasons for failure of 'good governance'. First, disputes about governance indicators are "endemically ideological." Measurement and selection of indicators are based on public administration and political frameworks. In this case the same indicator may have divergent interpretations depending on which ideological underpinning is utilised.

Second, some regimes forced into compliance by trade and aid considerations and they are simultaneously reluctant to produce and disseminate governance indicators that reflect adversely on the progress toward 'good governance'. This reluctance is compounded when indicators are used in cross-country comparisons and rankings.

Good governance is by and large treated as an instrumental value. According to stakeholders, it is a means by which to achieve a desired ends. Regarding good governance sometimes it means "Governance for poverty reduction" or "Governance for economic development/ efficiency".

The Human Rights Centre, University of Essex, issued a major report in 2003 on "Map-Making and Analysis of the Main International Initiatives on Developing Indicators on Democracy and Good Governance." The project, conducted by a team led by Todd Landman, was commissioned by the Statistical Office of the Commission of the European Communities (EUROSTAT). After completion of the project where different approaches and methodological options available for measuring democracy and good governance, the Final Report acknowledges from the outset, "however, that good governance remains an "essentially contested concept," since there is no consensus on its definition or content (Landman et al., p. 1). Different definitions lead to different measures of the concept. In the absence of a clear conceptual framework, controversy surrounds the tools of measurement".

The notion of 'good governance' will help in reforming governance of Bangladesh's institutions and organisations in some extent. To place right persons in right place is the issue of the day now in Bangladesh. Since the world it is a global village now it is acceptable to receive assistance and cooperation for reform of the governance flourish democracy. I shall be reasonable and critical as well while do research the issue of 'good governance'. Indeed my emphasis is to find out the root causes where Bangladesh fails again and again to follow the right path of democracy. By this, the research will help to establish right standard way of method where Bangladesh fits in.

What brought army to power?

In brief, this research has different hindrances of different categories:

Institutional hindrances are directly related to path-dependency and institutionalism approach. These include lack of Government neutrality, role of judiciary and law enforcement and de-centralisation.

Mistrust, suspicion, discord and crisis of identity are historical legacy. Some of them begun from colonial legacy and war of secession and some others started with restoration of democracy in 1991. Followed by 2007 military intervention the political crisis has been created centring 'Caretaker Government' issue again. In Bangladesh politics, individual (agent-centred) hindrances are sometimes related to political decisions and path-dependency as well.

Corruption is an issue which instigates army to take over power. However, these military motivations go against them when their people involve themselves into it. Sometimes, military thinks that it is 'saving' democracy by intervening into politics. Military coup of 1982 and 2007-08 military backed rules publicised this conception.

References

Ahamed, Emajudiin. 1988, Military Rule and Myths of democracy (Dhaka: Universitv Press, 1988).

Ahmed, Moudud. 1995, 'Democracy and the Challenge of Development – A Study of Politics and Military Interventions in Bangladesh'm UPL, Dhaka, Bangladesh.

Bertocci, Peter J., 1982. "Bangladesh in the Early 1980s: Praetorian Politics in an Intermediate Regime," Asian Survey 22. No 10 (October 1982).

Chowdhury, MMR. 2013. "Political Deadlock: Will History Repeat Itself In Bangladesh"?. Countercurrents.org. 30 December, 2013. Retrieved on 9 March 2014.

Dowse, Robert E. 1969. "The Military in Political Development," in

Polin'cr and Chrmge in Developing Counhies. cd. Colin Lqs (Cam-

bridge: CambridgeUniversity Pres, 1969).

Franda, Marcus. 1982, Bangladesh: The First Decade (New Delhi South

Asian Publishers, 1982), p. 50.

Feit, Edward. 1968 "Military Coup and Political Development," World

Politics 20, no 2 (1968).

Finer, The Man on Horsebock.

Ghoshal, Baladas. 2009, India Quarterly: A Journal of International Affairs 01/2009; 65(1):67-82.DOI:10 1177/097492840906500106

Hassan Uzzaman, l991. Bangladesh: Rastra O Sarkarer Samarikikaran (Bangladesh: Militarization of the state and government), Dhaka: University Press.

Huntington, Samuel. 1968, Political Order in Changing Societies (New

Haven: Yale University Press. 1968).

Jahan, Rounaq. Bangladesh Politics: Problems and Issues (Dhaka:

University Press, 1980), p. 115.

Janowitz, Morris, 1964. The Military in the Political Development of New

Nation (Chicago: Chicago University Press, 1964).

Khan, Zillur Rahman. 1984, Martial Law to Martial Law: Leadership Crisis in Bangladesh (Dhaka: University Press, 1984). p. 133.

Lifschultz, Lawrence. 1979, Bangladesh: Unfinished Revolution, London: Z Books.

Maniruzzaman, Talukdar. 1975, "Bangladesh: An Unfinished Revolution", Journal of Asian Studies 34,110.4 (August 1975): 891-910

Mastoor , Maryam. 2009, Bangladesh's Political Turmoil 2006-08: An Analysis, Regional Studies, XXXVII, No. 4, Autumn 2009, pg82-103

Pye, Lucian. 1962 "Armies in the Process of Political Modernization," in

The Role of Military in Underdeveloped countries, ed. John A Johnson

(Princeton: Princeton University Press, 1962).

Chapter 3

External Relations And Army's Role In Politics Of Bangladesh

By M Mukhlesur Rahman Chowdhury

07 January, 2015

An external relation has been playing one of the major roles in politics of Bangladesh. To make it clear, international actors' are very active there. In other words, Bangladesh has been an example where politics and international relations work together with evidence. It is obvious that the country gave its birth due to denial of democracy. The endless struggle for democracy still continues. The Western world and India are not only playing major role in Bangladesh politics but also they have their opinion for military rule in this territory as well. Since independence external relations are very much effective in this 8th largest country in the world. India, known as the largest democracy, surrounded Bangladesh in three sides. The only super power America matters in formulation of various policies in Bangladesh. Asian country Japan, an economic giant of the world, is the largest development partner of Bangladesh. The world's largest nation China, situated in Asia, is also a big seller of arms and ammunitions to Bangladesh. Russia, a country located mostly in Asia and also covered Europe, has been building nuclear power plant at 'Rooppur' in the country. Earlier it purchased Mig 29 from the then Soviet Union, now Russia.

Liberation war and Army started their journey in Bangladesh simultaneously. Track record shows, Army was involved in all kind of changeovers there since 1971, when the country came into being through its liberation war. During the liberation war, the government in exile worked from India. Expatriate Bangladeshis vigorously worked from the United Kingdom-UK for the cause of independence. British parliamentarians supported the cause of Bangladeshis freedom struggle strongly. Following the changeover of 1975, the United States of America-USA and part of Western world with China recognised Bangladesh. In 1982, India welcomed the changeover through Army coup in the country. Prior to fall of Ershad regime in 1990, top leaders of two rival political parties used to meet American Ambassador in Dhaka frequently. They had been parleying with visiting American diplomats to start with democracy. Thus Western world and Army's role were visible in all changeovers.

During 1971 war the USA wanted to send 7th fleet of its naval force to Bangladesh in favour of Pakistan when it was fighting against its previous country. Immediate after the independence, Bangladesh was in Soviet bloc. Bangladesh signed 25 years friendship treaty with India after independence. Then India had another treaty of similar kind with the Soviet Union. After the regime change in 1975, Bangladesh joined American and Chinese bloc. Recently Bangladesh received more areas through UN courts in its Bay of Bengal from Myanmar and India, which has been disputed for long time. It may be mentioned, Bangladesh is located in an important strategic location of South Asia, where India and China's eyes are open. As this century is for Asia, especially for South Asia, the USA is also very keen for this region and thereby for Bangladesh due to obvious reasons. World's one-fifth population lives in South Asia. Hence, South Asian Association for Regional Cooperation (SAARC) can be made a strong institute to harness the World's this important area's potential

It is widely believed that in Bangladesh governance, the Western world and India's influence matter. Following the military takeover by Lt. General Moeen U. Ahmed on 11 January 2007, former World Bank official Dr. Fakhruddin Ahmed was appointed the head of the government the next day, where the reason was to show that they received foreign powers support. In order to establish the same idea the military authority tried to make Bangladeshi noble laureate Dr. Muhammad Yunus the governmental head. Until eighties Bangladeshi military governments were backed by the western countries. Then there was a bi-polar world. However, usually in the present uni-polar world military takeover has been unlikely.

India helped Bangladesh in liberation war. On some occasions, India proposed name of Army Chief prior to announcement of such new appointment in Bangladesh. That indicates that India has a say even on military affairs of Bangladesh. In addition, during surrender of Pakistani Army on 16

December 1971 following victory of Bangladesh's liberation war Commander-in Chief General M. A. G. Osmani was not allowed to attend the ceremony. Later arrested all Pakistani Army personnel were released, pardoned and repatriated through Simla tri-party agreement under Indian initiative.

Bangladesh signed TICFA agreement with USA in 2013. Previously it signed another treaty called SOFA. China made a number of bridges in Bangladesh out of friendship and Japan also built airport, EPZ and other infrastructures. Korea invested in EPZ. It is estimated that more than three million Bangladeshi people live in the Kingdom of Saudi Arabia-KSA. Approximately seven million Bangladeshis live in Middle Eastern countries. More than ten million Bangladeshis live and work outside the country including the US, the UK and other European and Middle Eastern countries. Foreign remittance is one of the major sources of Bangladeshi wealth. Participation in UN Peace Keeping Force earns a good amount for defence and police people of Bangladesh as the country is pioneer for this mission.

Third generation Bangladeshi are doing well in Western countries such as the USA, the UK, Canada, Australia and some European countries. Last year at amid allegation of alleged corruption attempt, the World Bank suspended financing in the biggest development project 'Padma Bridge' in Bangladesh, which eventually led to withdrawal of loan proposal by the host country. Consequently, Bangladesh began the project with its own money. Prime Minister Sheikh Hasina, indicating the US, recently commented 'if one country does not support us, there are many countries around the World'. Earlier she remarked that she did not honour request of the US Secretary of State John Kerry and the UN secretary General Ban Ki-Moon in stopping Kader Molla's death sentence on his alleged involvement of war crime in 1971. PM and AL President Sheikh Hasina also informed that US State Department stopped World Bank funding to 'Padma Bridge'. However, America refused this allegation. Besides, present government received assistance from Japan for the development projects by extending its support for the country's candidature in the UN Security Council with withdrawing Bangladesh's nomination. Similarly it gave projects to China, Russia, Korea, Malaysia and the UAE. On the other hand, rest of the world including Western world do not support the 2014 election and thereby the present government. Due to this reason, the government has been facing image crisis. Therefore, the PM is visiting some countries and pursuing diplomacy through international relations. Likewise, an alliance namely 20 Parties comprising mainstream opposition political parties led by former Prime Minister Khaleda Zia are also pursuing their diplomacy with the UN, the USA, the UK and other development partners and countries. Thus both politics and international relations go side by side.

Bangladesh saw the end of military rule in 1990 through a mass upsurge. Since then it has been argued that possibilities of military intervention are very unlikely in the country. Some Bangladeshi political parties took advantage of this. They organised destructive political programmes such as blockade, demonstration with indigenous weapons namely 'Logi-Boitha' (Paddle-Stick), which created such a situation for military intervention with the military instigation as well that coincided their both individual and corporate interests (Chowdhury 2013). Due to this reason initially a large number of people welcomed the military intervention in 2007. A group of army worked behind the scene since 2002 by doing 'clean heart operation' under democratic regime (Asian Human Rights Commission 2002). Since then overtly or covertly army is backing the government to run the country. Later the force managed 2008 and 2014 disputed elections and keeping the government in power by suppression, oppression, killing, abducting and using arms by the government and political machinery. In the changed global scenario with threat of losing the prevailing facilities for army personals in UN Peace Keeping Force the scope of coup has been very thin and risky. The Economist (2007) headlined 'the coup that dare not speak its name', 'the army, not the politicians now runs Bangladesh'. 2007 coup was an exception and unique due to its failure in achieving its main target of army chief's becoming president even after two years of absolute army rule and due to its safe landing by handing over power through an arranged and 'disputed' election controlled by army. Thus the changeover in 2007 brought initially Army and eventually Awami League to power.

On the eve of military coup in 2007, it was seen that the foreign diplomats' posted in Bangladesh exercise excessive power. It helped to create lawlessness in the country, in fact, that helped military leaders to capitalise the created situation in their favour. There was a diplomatic club in Bangladesh comprises foreign diplomats stationed in Dhaka namely the Tuesday group was over active. Canadian High Commissioner Barbara Richardson, British High Commissioner Anwar Choudhury, who was of Bangladeshi origin and European Union's over publicised role also helped Army Chief to implement his mission. EU could not show that whatever they were doing that was in favour of democracy. Australian High Commissioner Douglas Fosket showed that his country was committed to democracy. The Bangladeshi Army group recorded some activities of foreign diplomats including US Ambassador's private activities, reportedly, to blackmail then.

With Western contradictory role and too much involvement in Bangladesh politics with no direction, the Army Chief Lt. Gen. Moeen U Ahmed declared the State of Emergency. He forced the President of Bangladesh Professor Dr. Iajuddin Ahmed to promulgate this at gun point. Then the Western world including the US and the UK were against military takeover and in favour of democracy. The military chief managed India, but it could not act openly due to the US's objection. UN resident Coordinator in Dhaka Renata Lok Dessallien took Moeen's side. She issued a letter what was sought by Moeen, That helped him to takeover although the UN Secretary General and UN Headquarters played the role in favour of democracy (Chowdhury 2014).

Renata helped directly and western world's role helped Moeen indirectly to capture the power. Finally the State of Emergency was declared and democracy was abrogated, the process of which was started in 1991. It has been argued that America did nothing to stop it. It gave only leap service, maintained liaison with all the contested parties and showed that they were in favour of democracy. But the end result is they did not do anything against military takeover. They probably made them agree to hold an election but the army held the election in such a way that AL comes to power. America knew the Indian role in Bangladesh. Evidence wise, India supported the army with supplying forces recently, for instance, a massacre was done in Satkhira jointly last year, intelligence gives service over DGFI, and for example, they are advising who will be the Army Chief in Bangladesh. As opposition claims, the country is helping with money and intelligence reports. Regardless which party in power in India they help Awami League in Bangladesh and the relation is not country to country, but country to party.

Regarding the role of think-tank of the USA, former ambassador to Bangladesh William B. Milam supported last army rule in a way by saying the politicians created the crisis. Critics argue about the mindset of the American, when another former ambassador Harry K Thomas was also not happy with immediate past government in Bangladesh. However, Harry has his own argument in this regard. Last US Ambassador Dan W. Mozena visited India and discussed Bangladesh issues with Indian government as he was assigned. An Indian lobby wants that USA should maintain relation with Bangladesh through them, which has not been accepted by the only superpower. British government's decision to issue visas on Bangladeshis passports in New Delhi created another issue among Bangladeshis as there are strong anti-Indian sentiments in Bangladesh for abovementioned reasons. In latest instance, India helped Awami League to continue in power with an election, organised by DGFI, by passing major political parties (Chowdhury 2014).

Defying visible role of the Western world at the end Army Chief took over, ruled the country for two years and made all efforts to become the President of the country and extended his tenure for one year and prior to his retirement. Consequently he could escape through handing over power to the Awami League with an arrangement of a managed election. The military continues playing their role so that the government remains in power since then. As a result, the western world's role against military intervention became only a leap service.

Since 2007 Bangladesh followed same policy during the Army and Awami League regimes. Both elections in 2008 and 2014 were, reportedly, conducted by Army with help from India. In 2014, the UN envoy Oscar Farnandez- Taranco was given commitment by the AL leaders including Tofail Ahmed and Amir Hossain Amu that there will be another election soon after the election of 5 January. They told for the sake of continuity of constitutional rule they had to follow, which was compared by them with March 1988 and February 1966 one sided elections. Another senior AL leader Finance Minister of AL government Abul Maal Abdul Muhit said, 5 January election was a third class election and they will hold another good election soon. The UN was blackmailed there. India requested the USA, the UN and other Western countries to allow the election to be held saying there will be another election soon after the so called one sided election boycotted by opposition parties. Followed by the election, India said it is Bangladesh's internal affairs. By the time, government has been changed and policy remained. President of India Pranab Mukherjee and Indian High Commissioner Pankaj Saran remained and they have say on this. It is reported that Indian intelligence people are working in Bangladesh intelligence agencies in some good positions.

In conclusion, Bangladeshi politicians did not take lesson from history. As far as military intervention is concerned, it has been argued that history repeats itself in Bangladesh (International Crisis Group, 2013), when it is inevitable.

Bibliography

Chowdhury, M Mukhlesur Rahman. (2014). USA's Efforts For A New Election To Restore Democracy In Bangladesh. Countercurrents.org 15 February 2014

Chowdhury, M Mukhlesur Rahman. (2014). Good Governance In Bangladesh: A Quest For Democracy. Countercurrents.org 19 January, 2014

Chowdhury, M Mukhlesur Rahman. (2014). Why The Military Intervened In Bangladesh Politics? Countercurrents.org 10 January, 2014

Chowdhury, M Mukhlesur Rahman. (2013). Political Deadlock: Will History Repeat Itself In Bangladesh? Countercurrents.org 30 December, 2013

Chowdhury, M Mukhlesur Rahman, (2010). Iajuddin was forced to promulgate emergency: Mukhles the Independent,Dhaka Friday 12 March 2010

Daily Star, (2006). UN concerned about free, fair polls in Bangladesh
Annan's special envoy meets Iajuddin, Hasina. Unb, Dhaka 30 November 2006 found
at**http://archive.thedailystar.net/2006/11/30/d6113001044.htm**

Daily Star, (2006). Military intervention won't help elections
Boucher says CG & EC must act neutrally 12 November 2006 found
at**http://archive.thedailystar.net/2006/11/12/d6111201033.htm**
Daily Star (2006). CA's resignation 'impractical'
Says US envoy 14 December 2006. Available
at**http://archive.thedailystar.net/2006/12/14/d61214012615.htm**

Daily Star, (2006) Nicholas Burns on Bangladesh. 30 November 2006 available
at**http://www.thedailystar.net/2006/11/30/d6113001033.htm**

International Crisis Group, (2013) Bangladesh: Back to the Future 13 June 2012 found
at**http://www.crisisgroup.org/en/regions/asia/south-asia/bangladesh/226-bangladesh-back-to-the-future.aspx**

Ittefaq, (2014). Samorik Shashon Jari Korte Cheyechhilen General Moeen Rastroptio Sabek Upodeshta Mokhlesur Rahmaner Sakkhatkar. 30 November 2014 Found
at**http://www.ittefaq.com.bd/print-edition/first-page/2014/11/30/17702.html**

Ittefaq, (2006). Ittefaq, (2006). 'Obadh O Shantipurno Nirbachon Onushthane Sobrokom Podokkhep Neaya Hoyecche – Jatisongho Bishesh Dutke Rashtropoti'**http://www.ittefaq.com.bd/print-edition/first-page/2014/11/30/17702.html**

The Economist (2007) 'The coup that dare not speak its name', 18 January 2007 found
at**http://www.economist.com/node/8560006**

Chapter 4

Good Governance In Bangladesh: A Quest For Democracy

By M Mukhlesur Rahman Chowdhury

19 January, 2014

1.0 Introduction

The quest for democracy in Bangladesh is moving in circles. The country gained its independence through both the democratic process and through war. During the four decades of its existence as a nation-state it has endured spells of military and non-military rules. Of the latter all were not elected and the elected governments themselves seemed to betray a superficial and perfunctory commitment to the norms and practices of democracy (Islam, 2004a).

Bangladesh's current debate of politics relates to the way the Caretaker Government (CTG), which started in 1991, raised issues of mistrust, suspicion, discord and enmity in politics. Such concerns have coloured Bangladeshi politics throughout the period to 2011, at which point the CTG was abolished (CNN, 2011; Hanley, 2005). The sitting government succeeded a military backed civilian caretaker government which took over amidst violent feuds among the sitting government and the opposition on the questions of the leadership of the mandatory pre-election caretaker (itself an invention introduced to forestall electoral malpractices by the sitting government), the membership of the election commission, voter list and even the type of ballot-boxes to be used (Khan, 2011). As if this is not enough the present sitting government at whose insistence, when in opposition, the novelty of pre-election caretaker government was introduced has made a complete volte face on its own invention, whereas the then sitting government, now the opposition, has vowed to boycott any election under its opponent. It underscores a thin and brittle veneer of democracy and a potential lurch towards an unelected government yet again. In this connection it is worth noting that the crusader of democracy who founded the nation-state and setup the multiparty parliamentary democracy had no less spectacular volte face; for with three years they opted for a one party dictatorship (Osman, 2010)!

Under the present world system based on nation-state representative democracy is indispensable. The question is what lay behind this apparent inability of the Bangladesh political classes to practice and sustain democracy (Kelly and Ashiagbor, 2013; Daily Star, 2012b).

This chapter is divided into four main parts. The first part of this paper is an overview of various academic theories and definitions of 'democracy' and specifically 'consolidated democracy'. The second part consists of a narrative history of Bangladeshi democratisation and governance. The third part presents introduction to historical institutionalism and idea of 'path dependency'. The fourth part provides the introduction to factors in Bangladesh that hinder democratic development (i.e. path dependencies, or may be results of path dependencies). A final part (conclusion) summarises with suggestions of solution to the problems of democracy and good governance in Bangladesh.

Part 1
1.1 Theoretical perspectives

This part aims to present an overview of various academic theories and definitions of 'democracy' and specifically 'consolidated democracy'. There is no universally agreed definition of democracy. However, it has been the most traded phenomenon in the worldwide political marketplace. Across the countries politicians use this notion in running the statecraft or governance for various reasons. Sometimes it has been used for right purpose and sometimes wrong. This term has been used as the catchword of political discourse (Schmitter and Karl 1991). "Today liberal democracy is the 'only game in town' (Chowdhury, 2011; Motohi, 2002); but we are free, of course, to play it badly" (Sartori 1991). Since beginning phrase of democracy echoes in the mind of people and resounds in their lips. People struggle for democracy to find freedom and a better way of life (Ibid). Bangladeshi people's struggle for democracy is relentless (Maniruzzaman, 1990).

Most authors (Mahoney, 2001; Milam, 2009) emphasise on three main elements of democracy. They are freedom or liberty, free and fair elections and meaningful political competition. Democratic structure needs to ensure "integrity of political competition and participation" (Hagerty, 2007). Indeed, democracy is a system of power sharing with all groups. As far as decision making is concerned it acts as a political force with authority. Linz argues, there is no alternative to institutionalisation of democracy, where all major actors, parties, or organised interests, forces or institutions involve (Linz and Stephan 1997; Hossain and Siddique, 2006). Contrarily, Harriss (2006) defined; democracy is consolidated only when all major groups come to both accept and defend democratic rules and procedures.

The system was not designed to meet the requirements of the state and people of Bangladesh. Centralisation and decentralisation's meaning is disputed (Smith, 1985). Pluralists value decentralisation as a virtue in all major forms. Tocqueville argues decentralised legal authority of federal constitutions (Datta, 2005).

Fakhrul (2002) evaluates, history of democracy begins in 1776. It coincided with American Revolution. Dahl considers democracy as an idea of representation. For Diamond and Morlino, "tend to move together democratic improvements and deepening or toward decay" (Grugel, 2002).

In the long run democracy is the safest means to solve the problems. People have been facing e.g. lack of decentralisation, corruption, ineffective parliament, violence, discord, mistrust and enmity (Chowdhury, 2011). There is a school of thought that argues democracy in a society such as Bangladesh exacerbates rather than resolves problems. There is a question whether there is one common model of democracy that fits every society (Devin, 2008). Sometimes benevolent dictators run the country better. Good governance can exist even in non-democratic regimes (Hall and Taylor, 1996).

'Good' governance is an essential prerequisite for any country. Governance includes sound development management in relation to public sector management, accountability, the legal framework for development and information and transparency (Haq, 2010). Donors and development partners use the word 'good' with governance since 80's. World Bank uses this term since 1978 (Chowdhury, 2008a). It classified good governance and poor governance in the sense of both effective and ineffective performances of the governments. Ideal and satisfactory system of government has also been as good governance (Chowdhury, 2007a).

Failure of politicians to establish good governance results in military intervention. Although military often play role in governance e.g. military personnel used to work for checking terrorism, anti-corruption drive, flood and cyclone control, building infra-structure and bridges even sometimes work to ease worst traffic situation.

CMR- Civil Military relations mean a relation between civilian political government and the military. Military's intervention into politics is another dimension in Bangladesh. There are three views on CMR (Anisuzzaman, 2000). The first view considers military as an apolitical and conservative force, which is untrained to involve in civilian rule as well as political management. However, it added that military has an inherent institutional desire to serve its corporate interest. For this reason it is incapable to lead the modernised nations. Lieuwen asserts that military is not a force for change (Chapman, 1990). Baxter (1992) supports this argument. He emphasizes distinction between modernisation and development. The development involves the building of political institutions, which is far away from military rule.

Bassford (1994) and Perrow (2006) agreed about the younger military officer's effort of reform and attempt to make some changes to alter present situations slightly. However, the changes may not occur finally, he admitted. Bangladesh's 1982 military intervention showed same thing where young military officers tried to reform political organisations and government institutions (Baxter, 1991).

A second view argues that revolution is the only mechanism. Development and reform can be brought under this initiative (Ahmed, 2003). It argues that regular military is the principal obstacle to this process in developing nations. In this argument scholars compared with Latin America's military interventions (Ahmed, 1994). In spite of differences of opinion to the main thrust, this view is partly related to the first opinion of military conservatism. It rejects the notion that developing countries military is capable of real development and stressed a neo-Marxist viewpoint. Huntington (1991) and Hossain and Siddique (2004) experimented on this thought in Latin America. They thought military is dependent on 'big powers' for military equipments and trainings. Hadenious (1997) believes African military is reactionary. However, he gives good marks to Congo-Brazzaville and military rulers of Ethiopia Marxist orientation. On the other hand, Jahan (2008) expresses high expectation about African military saying that this force is more effective than political parties.

Finally, according to the third view, military values, skills, ideologies are the antithesis of the first. As this opinion stands: military politicians in the developing countries (third world) would make the best as they are the reliable manager to change the society. Khan (1989) and Kochanek (1998) are supporters of military rule in the under-developed countries (third world). Among others, Shils (1962) and Johnson (1964) are in favour of this view. On the contrary, Lifschultz, (1979) is not convinced about military's capability to run the country for long time.

Generally CMR in democracy especially in an electoral political order is not always democratic. However, 'it has been a growth-industry in illiberal democracies' (Zakaria, 1997a).

Military interventions in politics began on the earth before last century. From the period of ancient Greece up to twentieth century, the displacement or the threat for displacement of an elected government by overt military action has been a recurrent theme in academic literature. Previously analysts looked at military institution as 'an alien and demonic', after the Second World War political scientists viewed it differently. It was argued that 'a military man cannot be a good man' (Zafarullah, 1996).

Riaz (2003) tried to overcome Huntington's model's limitations and differentiated civil-military relations in western countries from others. He made western countries CMR into three categories as aristocratic, democratic and totalitarian while for peripheral states it was classified into five categories e.g. authoritarian-personal, authoritarian-mass, democratic- competitive, civil-military coalition and military oligarchy (Momen, 2008). His typology has the problem that it does not consider civilian leaders degree of autonomy given by the military.

On the contrary, Momen's typology consists of three factors: the strength and weakness of civilian institutions, the strength and weakness of military institutions and the coercive, political and organisational resources at their disposal and the nature of the boundaries between the military establishment and its socio-political environment (Murshid, 2008).

Momen's typology has a problem that it neglects the role of international political, economic and military role on a country's civil-military relations (Rahman 2007b) gave supplementary definition. He found three types military intervention: one, military behind the government, two, after overthrowing civilian government military's short period regime and the last one is an ambitious group wants to do politics with agenda of society's reform (Rashiduzzaman, 2001a). Karabelias (1998) classified four types of military regimes. They are veto, moderator, factional and breakthrough. The next part looks into Bangladesh's democratic and governance position in the context of above theories.

Part 2
1.2 Democracy in Bangladesh

This part states narrative history of Bangladeshi democratisation and governance. It analyses the politics of Bangladesh and democratic problems during various regimes. Democracy is not a 'yes or no' question. It is complicated and changes with time. Bangladesh joined Huntington (1991) "third wave of democracy" after ousting extra- constitutional military backed government in January 2009. The country had joined similar situation in 1990 toppling another military regime of 9 years (Jahan 2008). Bangladesh witnessed various types of governance including Parliamentary, Presidential,

Caretaker Government (CTG) and Military form. Yet the country is in trial and error system of democracy (Islam, 2005a).

In Bangladesh, political organisations and government institutions are not following standard procedure. Country's human Rights situation is a serious issue (IDEA, 2006). Governance in Bangladesh lies with ruling party where opposition does not have a say. Always ruling party governed alone and opposition fights on the street. Both the parties demonstrate the same to meet their demand as opposition and oppose in same way while in the government (Islam, 2004b).

Bangladesh is a people's republic, although people have only a say on the day of election every after 5 years (Schaffer, 2002). However, that special day which still keeps the democratic process in the country, but in a vulnerable position. Bangladeshi people's constitutional rights to practice democracy in each and every tier of the administration are yet to be achieved (Schaffer, 2002).

After independence, democracy was buried by politicians and one party rule began (Talbot, 1998). It was followed by military takeover. The main leader's enormous charisma was matched with unsound vision of Bangladeshi people in the post liberation era (Thelen, 2004).

Following independence in 1971 ruling Awami League adopted Bangladesh's constitution with basic principles of Bengalee nationalism, parliamentary democracy, socialism and secularism in 1972 (Zakaria, 1997b). First leadership under Sheikh Mujibur Rahman amended the constitution to the one party rule with Presidential system in 1975. The authoritarian system curtailed people's right, freedom and liberties with abolishment of democracy. Later it was followed by a change over by dissident group of same party and then by military rule until 1979 (Stern, 2001). Three main leaders Sheikh Mujibur Rahman, Ziaur Rahman and Hussain Muhammd Ershad ruled the country from 1972 to 1990 (Rashiduzzaman, 2001b). Their founded parties Awami League, Bangladesh Nationalist Pary (BNP) and Jatiya Party (JP) are the mainstream parties in Bangladesh. Fourth biggest party is Jamaat-e Islami. After Mujib, Zia and Ershad's regimes, BNP and Awami League are in the helms of affair of Bangladesh governance again from 1991 to till date under the leadership of Begum Khaleda Zia and Sheikh Hasina Wajed respectively. They represent late Mujib and late Zia and have been leading two cults in the country (Przeworski, 1996).

After Sheikh Mujib, Ziaur Rahman emerged as leader of the country and amended the constitution. The basic two principles Bengalee nationalism and secularism were replaced by Bangladeshi Nationalism and the majority's value and culture Islamic ideals respectively while principle socialism was renamed as social justice (Rahaman, 2010). In the backdrop of the political scenario of Bangladesh, country has been divided into two blocks. Although all the parties are more or less agreed that Bangladesh should be governed based on majorities' opinion, value, belief and culture, still there is confusion on nationalism and belief (Rockman, 2000). Controversy has now been minimised by ruling party with adoption of State Religion and Bangladeshi nationality (Riaz, 2005). Awami League maintains relations with secularism and Islam as well as Bengalee and Bangladeshi simultaneously for mere political benefit to win over the voters (Steinmo, 1992).

Prime Minister Sheikh Hasina is the daughter of late President Sheikh Mujibur Rahman while former Prime Minister (present leader of the opposition) Khaleda Zia is the wife of late President Ziaur Rahman. Apart from this legacy, former President H M Ershad still leads the third party JP and Jamaate Islami is the fourth largest party (Steinmo, 1992).

In Bangladesh democracy has been restored in 1991 (Rashiduzzaman, 1994). Simultaneously, it is threatened by confrontational politics since then. The country witnessed four general elections with an extra-constitutional period of army backed government for two years in 2007-08 period and with an abortive military coup in 1996. To ensure neutrality and fairness in elections political parties agreed to introduce CTG system constitutionally in 1996 (Rashiduzzaman, 1997). Power is fully centralised in the country. Bangladesh lacks parliamentary or joint ministerial responsibility. Rather it is termed as Prime Ministerial type of democracy which was inherited from earlier Presidential system (Daily Star, 2011). Parliamentary Standing Committees are almost non-functional. Constitutional bodies including Judiciary, Anti-Corruption Commission, Public Service Commission and Human Rights Commission became government tools instead of independent bodies (Khan, 2005). These institutions became more problematic in recent days.

From 1991 to 2006 there was a "minimalist democracy", where Bangladesh made gradual progress in respect to participatory elections, peaceful power transfer to majority party and continued civilian rule (Khan, 2011). Within this period, the country organised three elections in 1991, 1996 and 2001 respectively. International elections monitors and observers certified them as free and fair polls. Then many factors including army and international involvement ensured peaceful transfer of power (Islam, 2006). In between these periods military leaders were in favour of civilian control except only in 1996 Caretaker regime when there was an abortive military coup led by Lt. General A S M Nasim. That coup was failed as military leaders supported then President Abdur Rahman Biswas (Ittefaq, 1995).

Although there is a dispute about definition of democracy worldwide, the democracy is the safest way of governance where people can practice their rights. Good governance is essential prerequisite for democratic consolidation. There is no alternative to institutionalisation of democracy, where all major actors, parties, or organised interests, forces or institutions involve (ICISS, 2001).

Present political crisis started on 28 December, 1994 when after walk outs and long boycott as well as observing hartals and street agitation. Awami League led opposition parties MPs resigned en masse in protesting against 'rigging' in a bye-election of a parliamentary seat in a Magura constituency (Hasanuzzaman, 1998). Followed by the election, the demand came from then opposition parties to incorporate CTG in the constitution. To solve the deadlock situation then there was a mediation effort from Commonwealth Secretary General Chief Emeka Anyaoku, which failed finally (Ittefaq, 1995). Then as the special envoy of the Secretary General former Governor General and Justice of Australia Sir Ninian Stephen parleyed to solve that political crisis in vain. In that situation, opposition parties did not participate in the parliamentary election in 15 February 1996. Under the pressure from opposition, ruling BNP passed 13th amendment of the constitution on 26 March 1996, which introduced the Caretaker Government system during parliamentary election period. Besides, there was an election held under a consensus CTG in 1991 following the fall of military turned authoritarian rule. Under new system of non-party CTG the next election was held on 12 June 1996, where Awami League won. Like predecessor, new opposition BNP followed the path of Awami League in walk out and boycott, hartals and street violence (Hagerty, 2007). In the following elections of 2001 BNP and its allies gained a landslide victory. Awami League again started observing frequent hartals, agitation, boycott the parliament. AL was absent in parliament session of 2005 for 61 days out of 62 days (Islam, 2005b). Main issues of that political movement were who will be the next CTG chief, who will be Election Commissioners and who will have the defence ministry during CTG period (Islam, 2005).

Some new phenomenon added fuel to fire as government decided at least three issues, which was not accepted by opposition. They are increasing of Supreme Court Judges retirement age, government's refusal to allocate defense ministry to Chief Adviser of CTG instead of President and reconstitution of Election Commission issue. Awami League led opposition alleged that to make a pro-BNP man Justice K M Hassan the Chief Adviser the 14th amendment of the constitution was passed which increased retirement age of Supreme Court Judges, they did not accept the President as defence minister during CTG period and Justice M A Aziz as Chief Election Commissioner (CEC) (Daily Star, 2001). Opposition expressed doubt about a free and fair election to be held. Both main rivalry parties attended dialogue to solve crisis and they solved 30 issues but one, which was about CTG chief issue. Dialogue ended there. "Thus the next general election due to be held in January, 2007 looks little uncertain" (Chowdhury, 2010). Situation became volatile as opposition went for street violence again to meet their demand.

Awami League and their allies' organised countrywide blockade and violence with country made arms and weapons called 'Logi-Boitha' (indigenous stick and paddle used as weapons on the street) on 28 October which day was the last day of the BNP government's tenure (Chowdhury, 2011). As there was no solution of political stalemate in the worst situation the Chief Adviser in waiting Justice Hassan refused to take his constitutional responsibility. A dialogue was arranged between President and four major parties representing the parliament in order to agree to appoint a new CTG chief within the purview of the constitution. But arch-rival parties could not come to a solution. There were 5 options to appoint the CTG chief, which were exhausted for the non-co-operation of political parties. Finally the President had to take over as the Chief Adviser in addition to his responsibility in line with the sixth and the last option given in the constitution. CTG started its journey on 29 October 2006 (Daily Star, 2012b).

An army group tried to take power into their grief, wanted to hold one sided elections, instigate some parties to continue street violence, foiled CTG's army deployment in aid to civil power to restore law and order and planned to declare a state of emergency in disguise (Chowdhury 2007, 2008, Amar Desh 2008, Daily Star, 2011). President's Adviser Mukhlesur Rahman Chowdhury, who is the author of this research paper, mediated with two top leaders met their demands and brought all political parties into election by 26 December 2006 (Daily Star, 2012b). However, the army group with association of some political leaders managed to cancel Jatiya Party Chief H M Ershad's nomination. They created a situation where agitating parties withdrew en masse on 3 January 2007 from 22 January 2007's planned election competition (Independent, 2007). Finally, army chief and his group took over power on 11 January 2007 using the cancellation of JP Chairman's nomination as trump card (Daily Star, 2011).

Army chief failed to become the President of Bangladesh and had to go back to barrack after made a mess in Bangladesh governance. They tried to minus two top leaders, arrested hundreds of thousand leaders and made themselves involved in corruption instead of organise drive against this (Devin, 2008). Military-backed government ruled Bangladesh for two years and handed over power to Awami League through election. Military returned to barrack following international pressure and Moeen's proposal sent to USA State Department to switch over to Martial Law from State of Emergency was outright rejected (Chowdhury, 2008a; Daily Star, 2011). AL received more than three-fourth majority, which was unusual as Sheikh Hasina expected 160-170 seats in the 300 direct seats of parliament. Khaleda Zia alleged that in the army manipulated elections AL was given unusual seats in the parliament to amend the constitution in their favour. Khaleda Zia also claimed in a public meeting in 2009 about she refused an army formula where proposal was given that army chief and his associates those who were involved in 11 January military coup will not be tried and in return she has been assured that her party will be given three-fourth seats (Haq, 2010). On the other hand, Prime Minister Sheikh Hasina made comment that she could make third major party leader Ershad the opposition leader instead of Khaleda Zia (Daily Star, 2012b).

After two years of unconstitutional rule, although Bangladesh backed to democratic process but it follows same path of vengeance, violence, discord. Situation of human rights is serious. Army government's some good initiatives including reform in the various sectors and political organisations and government institutions were abandoned. Missing, disappearance, abduction and killing of opponent are everyday picture (Hanley, 2006). Moreover, ruling party AL abolished CTG system in 2011 unilaterally using a incomplete and short verdict of 'partisan' court (Khan, 2011). CTG was the last resort to check a minimal fair election where there was scope to change the government after 5 years, which has now gone (Moniruzzaman, 2009).

Bangladesh witnessed a result of civil-military relations while a new government emerged on 7 November 1975, when there was no-government situation prevailed in the country. The situation emerged through a combination of civil and military effort following series of military coups-counter coups (Maniruzzaman, 1990). Besides, CMR worked again in 1996 when civil bureaucrats came out to the street joining political platform 'Janatar Mancha' and a military coup happened afterwards. Similarity is civil and military forces worked together on the both occasions and dissimilarity is the first one was not directly under political party's leadership and second one was so (Motohi, 2002).

Bangladesh's current political situation has similarity with the situation of 2006 prior to military intervention occurred in 2007 that lasted until the beginning of 2009, a period of critical juncture. That period showed a path dependency which lasted for a longer time than the period of critical juncture (Osman, 2010).

Thus Bangladeshi process of democratic consolidation has again in a critical juncture. A simple issue of free and fair election created this situation. The issue is the centre point of historical forces. It shaped the present politics of the country (Rahaman, 2010). Continuation of this contentious politics can create a serious repercussion on the governance of Bangladesh. It can affect on economy as well as political stability in the country. Development partners are concerned for free and fair elections in Bangladesh and urged to have a mechanism to hold neutral and impartial administration to run the country during general elections and to stop human rights violation as well as political violence (Moniruzzaman, 2009). Due to crises Bangladesh has been facing critical junctures, where path dependencies occur as well (Khan, 2011).

Part 3
1.3 Historical Institutionalism (HI), Critical Juncture and Path dependency in Bangladesh

This part provides an introduction to historical institutionalism (HI) and idea of 'path dependency' with reference to critical juncture. HI is the one of the approaches in social sciences to understand politics. This approach needs to be looked into in a historical and comparative context. It also needs to see that where the approach was originated and how it is different from other approaches. HI approach has two important parts; critical junctures and path dependency (Khan, 2005).

Historical institutionalists stand between the two views: human beings are both norm abiding rule followers and self- interested rational actors. How one behaves depends on the individual, on the context and on the rule (Kochanek, 1998). Historical Institutionalism (HI) focuses well on institutions and the ways they change over time; traces path dependencies and the way that decisions and structures have long term effects; and makes very complex issues easier to understand (Lifschultz, 1979).

The hindrances to democracy in Bangladesh are potential sources or results of historical institutionalism path dependencies. Institutional hindrances are directly related to path-dependency and institutionalism approach. These are lack of Government neutrality, role of judiciary and law enforcement, decentralization. Military interventions happened as path dependencies. Political failures invite these interventions. Critical junctures and path dependency cycle in the country and path has not been shaped yet (Mahoney, 2001).

Cultural as well as social hindrances have been a result of previous political choices and events. So path dependency is relevant here too. Mistrust, suspicion, discord and crisis of identity are historical legacy. Some of them begun from colonial legacy and war of secession and some others started with restoration of democracy in 1991. Individual (agent-centred) hindrances are sometimes related to political decisions and path-dependency as well (Dyer, 2013).

Historical Institutionalism (HI) is appropriate in evaluating Bangladesh governance. Bangladesh has been witnessing many critical junctures, which ended in path dependency (Kochanek, 1998). The country now also faces a critical juncture based on Caretaker Government Issue during holding parliament elections as rivalry political parties are in daggers point. Limitation of HI is it does path dependence, but does not make path shaping. However, history matters in Bangladesh politics (Khan, 2011).

Historical Institutionalism (HI) provides a valid and powerful theory to evaluate the democratic development as well as legacies. Conception of HI is the policy choices of institution and its impact on future policy. The policy is based on long-range determining effect. This argument is called 'path dependency'. In other word, history matters as 'path dependency'. Path dependency does not mean the present and future is determined by past decisions. Past decision set the context in which contemporary decisions are taken (Islam, 2005b). This includes the decisions made both in statistical sense ('history matters') and in respect of chaos theory ('small changes matter'). For the HI approach Thelen (1991) has major contributions.

HI consists of historical legacy and persistence of institutions. The policy choices made when an institution was formulated or when new policy was initiated would have a persistent crucial influence over time. It is opposite to behaviouralism and rational choice theory (Hossain and Siddiquee, 2006). Sunk cost- the cost of constructing the existing arrangement or transaction cost of a new formation might prevent policy reform. Positive feedback effect is once new path-shaping occurred; actors strengthen the new system as well as adjust the new logic (Islam, 2004b).

In HI, institution is formal and organisational to informal and amorphous (e.g., rules, procedures, norms etc.). An institution is 'a collection of values and rules, largely normative rather than cognitive in the way in which they impact on institutional members as well as the routines that are developed and enforce those values' (Huq, 1973).

To analyse the theory it is essential to discuss the key themes of HI. It needs to see the explanations and responses of key themes of HI as well. The way changes occur in HI –Punctuated equilibrium: an equilibrium state of institutions in favour of initial institutional choice or previous punctuation (open to change if there is a substantial environmental change or pressure).

Critical juncture—existing path can be changed when inherent dilemmas occur or institutional arrangement has become undermined (at that time a window of opportunity is opened, and old and new factors begin to struggle over how to change current policy; the old path affects the shaping of the new path). Power distributional approach—political negotiation and transfer of coalitional foundation can make change. 'Historical institutionalists accepted the contention that conflict among rival groups for scarce resources lies at the heart of politics, but they sought better explanations for the distinctiveness of national political outcomes and for the inequalities that mark these outcomes' (Hall & Taylor 1996/6).

Individual's role –Traditional version: In HI the role of actors shrunk to a minimum. New explanations—political change can occur when there is a conflict of coalitions of actors seeking change or observation of the existing institution (IDEA, 2006). The role of ideas and cultures– Institutional transformation—ideas and cultures can formulate or change the preferences of individuals, which can crucially affect a transformation.

HI approach has some limits and weaknesses –HI only explains the past (cannot explain the present or predict the future) (Islam, 2004b). It is not good at explaining institutional performance or what a good institution is (main purpose of this approach is to institutional endurance and its policies rather than assess the performance of institutions, which is the main task of old version institutionalism). HI has difficulty explaining the role of agency (the traditional stance of HI puts structural constraints over agencies) (Allen, 1994).

1.3.1 Historical legacy

People of Bangladesh are almost homogeneous (ICISS, 2001). The country has colonial legacy and the legacy of the war of secession. Bangladesh does not have any sectarian, ethnic or communal problems. But the society and its culture are politicised (Ittefaq, 1975). Politics is divisive and based on grievances. Although political parties suffered a lot during the last military regime they failed to consolidate democracy. There is no co-operation between rivalry political parties. This political feature of vendettas can be termed as historical and ideological (Islam, 2004b).

Awami League finds it difficult to recognise BNP as a legitimate contender. It evaluated BNP is beneficiary following topple of AL. On the other hand, BNP observed that AL buried democracy with introduction of Bangladesh Krishak Sramik Awami League (BKSAL) and BNP reintroduced multi party democracy with new birth of AL in Bangladesh politics (Chowdhury, 2007a).

Bangladesh has been facing critical junctures through historical legacies, war and through political problems. Following critical junctures in 1975, 1981, 1990, 1996 and 2006, Bangladesh has been witnessed path dependencies which lasted longer period than the critical junctures occurred (Rockman, 2000; Rahman, 2007b). The country faced critical junctures in 1975, 1981, 1990, 1996 and in 2006 and during all periods political changes occurred and following path dependencies lasted longer than the period critical junctures. Bangladesh witnessed number of assassinations of top leaders through the result of path dependencies or result of path dependencies (Riaz, 2004; Sarmila, 2010).

Bangladeshi institutions were framed in the context of power relations as it has relevance with 'the rules of the game' (Stern, 2001). In Bangladesh formal institutionalism has taken place. Its parliamentary structure allows variations across the country. Personality cult remains in the country too. Unlike Africa (Erdmann et al 2011), Bangladesh lacks tribe system. Historical Institutionalism (HI) has been used in analysing the governance through democracy and dictatorship in various countries (Steinmo, 1992).

In the globalisation of politics, Bangladeshi political problems are now an international issue. Development partners and international agencies are concerned for Bangladesh's democratic development, good governance and corruption issue (Sarkar, 2008). World Bank recently stopped financing to Bangladesh projects due to alleged corruption of government (Daily Star, 2012a).

Historical legacies brought Bangladesh to the present situation with many developments (Momen, 2008).

Part 4
1.4 Obstacles to democratic consolidation

The fourth part engages in introduction to factors in Bangladesh that hinder democratic development (i.e. path dependencies, or maybe results of path dependencies). This section identifies a number of obstacles of Bangladesh's democracy. They are authoritarian governance, crisis of identity, enmity, violence, corruption, partisan bureaucracy and judiciary, ineffective parliament, caretaker government (CTG), external factors and military interventions.

1.4.1 Authoritarian governance

Bangladesh could not come out of some common problems and issues of different periods. These are mistrust, suspicion, discord, enmity and identity crisis (Murshid, 2008). Under the character of unitary constitution government is run by ruling party where the Prime Minister controls everything. Parliament and Cabinet do not function jointly according to the constitution. Nation has been facing the consequences of violence, vengeance and intransigence, which gradually became major characteristics of Bangladesh politics (Putnam, 1993).

The ruling party undertakes repressive measures to opponents in the form of legal and police repression. Debate, discussion, compromise, understanding and accommodation between ruling and opposition parties are absent In Bangladesh (Przeworski, 1999). A sense of vengeance and vendetta has been in the politics in the country. Moreover, a relationship of hatred in cyclic order between the political parties is manifested in Bangladesh politics (Chowdhury, 2011). This negative issue inevitably leads to standstill as far as debate and discussion are concerned over policy issues, which further widen the rift of the society (Chowdhury, 2010).

1.4.2 Crisis of identity

Nation is divided on nationality issue. Awami League believes in Bengalee nationalism, language based nationalism while BNP, JP and other parties believe in Bangladeshi nationalism, territorial nationalism. Basically, this created an identity crisis. Basically, Bangladesh constitution was hired from its Indian origin (Devin, 2008). After independence no innovative thing was done as far as constitution is concerned other than tinkering (Daily Star, 2007).

Regarding religion's role in politics, Awami League's official position is secularism. But for the voter sake this political organisation compromised with 'Bismillahir Rahmanir Rahim' (To start with all activities in the name of creator and lord Allah) in the preamble of the constitution, which was inducted by Zia and state religion incorporated by Ershad (Haque, 1981). In 2011, AL amended the constitution deleting one of the principles namely 'absolute faith and trust in almighty Allah' and it was replaced by secularism. Thus, constitution became now a self-contradictory document (Daily Star, 2012b).

1.4.3 Enmity

The thoughts of Bangladesh's top leadership have been dominated by a range of arrogance. An element of intolerance makes the mindset of leadership (IDEA, 2006). This way rivalry spreads in various political levels. One of the reasons of this rivalry is emergence enmity between political parties. The second reason stands opposition parties street politics. These discourses are related with historical perspective (Islam, 2005a).

Apart from historical legacy behind the rise of violence, two other factors contributed in this development (Islam, 2004b). They are emergence of enemy discourse between major parties and opposition party's demonstration in the street. Violence became one of the characteristics of the country's polity.

Enmity began with proclamation of independence in 1971. BNP has been observing that Major Zia declared independence when Sheikh Mujib was in Pakistani jail while AL does not want to give credit Zia (ICISS, 2001). It made permanent division in political arena. 'A Parliamentary Government requires a certain level of respect, consideration, and cooperation between the government and the opposition, and this includes consultation between the prime minister and the leader of opposition' (Jahan, 2000).

1.4.4 Violence

The hatred of political parties instigates violence in politics. Opposition parties as well as Human Rights organisations often complain that the government is using state apparatus to repress opponents. Gradually, this repression became 'legitimate' cause for violence. Disappearances, abduction and killings added new phenomenon in Bangladesh politics. Countrywide similar kind of incidents happened to 127 persons (Jahan, 2004). Using state machinery this sort of occurrence continues despite constant criticisms of the human rights organisations, donors and international organisations. Extortion and murder are also manifestation of violence. The former British High Commissioner to Bangladesh Stephan Evans stated, the politics of confrontation is the biggest threat to Bangladesh (Daily Star, 2011).

Hartal (General strike) is one of the major factors in Bangladesh politics since British period in India (1757-1947) (Jahan, 2003). This turned into violent shape in recent years. It causes confrontation between the parties. During various regime hartal has been a successful tool in ousting government. Political violence has another means of repression by state (Kochanek, 1998).

President Jimmy Carter of USA was assured by Bangladeshi political parties in 2001 that elections result will be accepted whatever the result would be and there will be no hartal. But later the thing went to the other direction (Mahoney, 2001).

1.4.5 Corruption

Corruption is another major problem for Bangladesh and an impediment towards development. Bureaucracy and judiciary are also affected by this (Motohi, 2002). Reason of absence of rule of law in Bangladesh is massive corruption. Bangladesh was ranked as the most corrupt country from 2001 to 2005 by Transparency International (TI) (Mohammad, 2008), which still continues although the situation has been improved. Successive governments used Anti-Corruption Commissions or Bureaus for partisan interest. World Bank stopped a major project of Padma Bridge in Bangladesh recently for alleged corruption of government (Daily Star, 2012b). Recently a section of politicians come from business class. Since the time of abolishment of Zamindari system in 1951, new elites from the business class started influence and later controlled the politics. At present, many of the elite politicians come from business sector (Momen, 2008).

1.4.6 Politicisation of administration

Unlike developed countries, bureaucracy and judiciary are handled by the government of the day. Due to this the government becomes weaker and non-participatory. Bureaucracy's neutrality and faceless position has been questioned. Politics divided Bangladesh bureaucracy. Promotion is based on political loyalty. Opponent officers are made OSD (Officer on Special Duty) for political reason (Murshid, 2008). Quality of bureaucracy and accountability has been affected by these malpractices.

A section of civil servants joined the 'Public Platform' (Janatar Mancha) on the street under the banner of political party AL in 1996 in order to topple BNP government on the eve of an abortive military coup (Ittefaq 1996).

1.4.7 Politically biased judiciary

Recently separation of judiciary has been done in Bangladesh. However, ruling party has monopolistic control over government machinery (Rockman, 2000). Its excess influence over judiciary is another obstacle of good governance (Moniruzzaman, 2009).

Two verdicts of Supreme Court are the manifestations of political biasness of judiciary. They are the verdict on the political issue of declaration of independence and about fundamentals of constitution with CTG system issue. "This partisan approach to law enforcement extends from top to the bottom of the political system and applies to the behaviour of both the parties when in office" (Rahman, 2007b).

1.4.8 Ineffective parliament

Both AL and BNP compromised for parliamentary system in 1991 (Rahman, 2007b). Contrarily, since then the boycott culture became a threat to parliamentary democracy. In the parliamentary sessions ruling party does not allow the opposition to criticise them or participate in any issue which embarrass them. On the other side, opposition parties used to attend parliament session before their membership expires in 90th consecutive day to retain their seats. This practice continues since in 1991 (Rashiduzzaman, 2001a). Centring an issue of rigging in a bye-election of a parliamentary seat the mainstream opposition parties resigned from the parliament in 1994 and since then streets have become the centre-point of politics instead of parliament in Bangladesh (Hasanuzzaman, 1998, Ahmed, 2003). Speaker is appointed from the ruling party (Bangladesh Constitution) and he does not act neutrally (Riaz, 2004).

1.4.9 Caretaker Government (CTG)

Bangladesh has been with the circles of CTG issue since 1991. There were demands from the political parties to improve this innovative system, whereas it was abolished in 2011 through the 15th amendment of the constitution (Sobhan, 2004). The ruling party's this decision created a critical juncture after three and half years rule of present government, when major political parties have been in the street movement following the political development. Future course of country's democracy and governance is again in uncertainty. In these circumstances, Bangladesh's democracy is termed as 'nothing but illiberal democracy' (Zakaria, 1997b). Although there is a provision to appoint ombudsman to oversee accountability of the government but it is yet to be established. Besides, there is no other institutional structure or system of this kind, which can solve the political crisis as a guardian (Haq, 2010).

1.4.10 External factors

Foreign intervention in domestic politics is an old phenomenon. Colonial legacy of various countries are manifestation of this intervention. In this globalisation era, external factors are also important for developing countries democracy. British colonial experience helped in reviving democracy in its some former colonies (Fakhrul, 2002). Donors especially World Bank (WB), International Monetary Fund (IMF), Asian Development Bank (ADB) and developed countries such as USA, UK and Japan give conditions to follow certain standards in Human Rights and good governance in providing aid and assistance to the developing countries (Grugel, 2002).

The world witnesses latest Egypt, Libya and Syria issue. Sometimes this intervention helps democracy and sometimes to the foreign countries as well as military or authoritarian government. USA, UK, UN, WB are watching Bangladesh situation and ask political parties to restrain from discord and violence (Daily Star, 2011; Chowdhury, 2011).

Sometimes, the role of external powers affects the internal configuration of politics in Bangladesh or other countries. Relations with external powers affect the policies of the political parties such as AL, BNP, JP and JI. Sometimes, these relations influence the outcomes of elections (Devin, 2008).

Commonwealth Secretary General Chief Emeka Anyaoku's special envoy Sir Ninian Stephen mediated Bangladesh political stalemate in 1995 (Chowdhury, 2010; Telegraph 1995). US President Jimmy Carter mediated with the Bangladeshi political parties on the eve of 2001 parliamentary election. During the volatile situation of 2006 western diplomats were very busy with Bangladeshi political leaders and government actors to overcome the deadlock occurred (Chowdhury, 2011; Daily Star, 2012b). UN Secretary General Kofi A Annan's special emissary Craig Gennes and US Assistant Secretary General Richard A Boucher and Under Secretary of State in the US State Department used their good offices as well to solve the political crisis as foreign actors (Datta, 2005). The role of British High Commissioner Anwar Chowdhury, Canadian High Commissioner Barbara Richardson and UN

Resident Representative Renata Lok Dessalien was 'controversial', which was well publicised in home and abroad.

1.4.11 Military intervention

In Bangladesh, relationships with the army in power sometimes influence the voting patterns. Economic downturn and lack of good governance make a government unpopular. In these circumstances it becomes difficult for an incumbent government to win an election (e.g. increasing price hike of essential commodities, deteriorating conditions of roads, infrastructures, acute crisis of electricity etc). As a result, as the incumbent government tries to stay in power they apply 'coercive methods' (money, muscle, government forces etc), which aggravates the conflict with the opposition (Haq, 2010).

Bangladeshi military has been engaged in United Nations (UN) Peace Keeping Force since late 80's that helped continuation of democracy in the country (Hagerty, 2007). Despite these achievements Bangladesh could not consolidate democratic institutions. Although military is not in power but autocratic system remains in civil leadership. Ruling party continues using state power for political supporters and opposition is repressed by government for political reasons.

Army has been playing a vital role in Bangladeshi governance since inception. The country's birth depends on a legacy of war, where army's role was pioneer. They played role in changing the governments during various authoritarian regimes as well. General H M Ershad, who took over power through a coup in 1982 proposed army's share in statecraft in a constitutional way. Like Ershad, General Moeen U Ahmed also wanted to form National Security Council (NSC) with army's involvement in administration (ICISS, 2001). Bangladesh army is a Pakistani legacy. It followed its predecessor's path in overthrowing elected governments. Militarisation, deputation and civilisation have been continuing in various regimes (Jahan 2008). Fourth amendment of the constitution buried constitutional democracy and pluralism. As a result, military became directly involved in politics through that amendment by joining one party BKSAL rule (Daily Star, 2012b, Jahan 2008). Presidential system also began by that system. Military did not continue its support for Ershad's regime after about 9 years of governance. Rather then it helped democratic transition in 1990. A group of military led by its chief General Nasim staged a coup in 1996, which was failed. In 2007 another coup led by Army Chief General Moeen U Ahmed overthrown a constitutional Caretaker Government (CTG) and ruled the country for two years. However, army chief did not succeed to become the President. Thus the aim of the coup failed (Islam, 2005a). The reason of failure of that coup was development partners and international world including USA, UN, Commonwealth and EU did not support martial law and army chief's intention to be the head of the state (Chowdhury 2007, Manabzamin 2007, Amar Desh 2008, Thikana 2008).

Army sought magistracy power several times as it was called in aid to civil power (Murshid, 2008) to maintain law and order, check terrorism, control flood, cyclone and tidal bore, and clean heart operation and even to manage worst traffic problem in the capital city. It makes army ambitious in running the statecraft. After collapses of Soviet Union and high risk of losing the role in UN Peace Keeping Force it is not possible like previously to overthrow the elected government.

A military intervention occurred in Bangladesh on 11 January 2007. After failing to declare Martial Law Army Chief Lt. General Moeen U Ahmed forced country's president to declare a State of Emergency (Rahaman, 2010). Army ruled the country for two years. Although a section of military wanted to reform Bangladesh politics and governance and to stop corruption, they failed when Army Chief tried to materialise his dream to be the President and a section of Army involved themselves in corruption. Earlier military intervention happened in liberation war in 1971, August and November in 1975, March 1982, December 1990 and May 1996 (Rockman, 2000; Rahman, 2007a). Military is called 'third force' in Bangladesh as it intervenes in politics. Sometimes, some small parties take effort to form a 'third force' (in political platform). Democratic behaviour of political parties can bring army under a system, which developed countries have been practicing for over the years (Murshid, 2008).

1.5 Conclusion

This chapter examined the reasons behind Bangladesh's confrontational politics. It has been seen that the political situation in Bangladesh does not equal any of the academic definitions of democracy at the moment. The unresolved issue of Caretaker Government (CTG) is manifestation of this mistrust, suspicion, discord and enmity have been characterised with political behaviour in the country. In some ways CTG was similar to this definition, because all parties agreed with the CTG system safeguarding elections as 'the only game in town' (Linz and Stephan 1997, Przerworski 1999). As the system later failed, this suggests that Huntington's definition of consolidated democracy is 'wrong' or 'weak'.

It has been seen that country became the victim of political division since 1991 and it continues until 2011. Recently the study of violence and killing has emerged as one of the major areas of research in political science as well as in the political sociology (Murshid, 2008). Entire periods are linked with the beginning and end of CTG system. With the end of this system, the political situation has further deteriorated. It is now essential to look at the context through an analytical framework.

It argues that Bangladesh has been facing problems of enmity between rival political parties, ineffective parliament and politics of street cause the violence, confrontation and discord. It has been found that the enmity is linked with ideological, cultural, historical and political dimensions. These issues instigate a political culture of intolerance, mistrust, and suspicion, which turn into antagonism. It creates arrogance and revenge as well. This leads to a situation of stalemate, deadlock and relations of non-cooperation among the parties. This is a cycle Bangladesh witnesses repeatedly. The issue of the ruling party's monopolistic attitude of governance, sense of deprivation of opposition parties inevitably brings debate and discussion on policy issues to a standstill. Finding no other alternatives, the opposition demonstrates their power on the street in order to compel the government to vow down to their pressure. Consequently, government tries to suppress and oppress the movement. As a result, these are reason of obvious confrontational consequence. This way history repeats itself in Bangladesh. By the time this became one of the characteristics of Bangladeshi politics. These problems are obstacles of institutionalisation of democracy, good governance, and economic development. On the other hand it causes human life and damage to properties.

Some scholars very recently started doing research activities to find out required reform for Bangladesh governance. It will help the country to pursue adequate reform programmes. Country like Bangladesh regularly has to meet many requirements to maintain its global relationship update and to cope with world standard. For example, recently Bangladesh had to introduce Machine Readable Passport (MRP) and Machine Readable Visa (MRV) system and signed treaty to join e-passport after 2014 in line with international requirement. Bangladesh had to restructure old model Anti-Corruption Bureau, which was replaced by Anti-Corruption Commission (ACC) under World Bank and other donors pressure in 1995. However, ACC could not start proper functioning due to wrong choice of its operator by the successive governments.

Bangladesh needs structural changes in the governance and parliament. Reform is essential outside parliament as well. Pierson (2004) argues, formal institutional change can induce informal changes in behaviour. For structural change Bangladesh needs both internal and external support. Civil society, media and international development partners can come forward to institutionalise democracy and establish good governance. As aid and assistance have links (Khan, 2011) with democracy and good governance, international donors can find a way to facilitate development of Bangladeshi system of governance. With this assistance the country can meet the criteria to join developed world from developing stage.

Bangladeshi democracy has been passing a critical juncture. However, recession in developed world could not affect Bangladesh. Country's economy is in better position as well as development is going on in social sectors, which is admirable too. Bangladesh needs institutionalisation of democracy and ensures good governance to overcome confrontational politics and to achieve faster economic development.

Chapter 5

Political Deadlock: Will History Repeat Itself In Bangladesh?

By M Mukhlesur Rahman Chowdhury

30 December, 2013

As the United Nations (UN) failed to solve the political crisis of Bangladesh with the end of recent fruitless discussions between the ruling Awami League (AL) and main opposition Bangladesh Nationalist Party (BNP), the trend of violence has been increasing. The manifestation of increased violence includes the attacks on Bangladesh Supreme Court, Jatiya Press Club and Dhaka University on 29 December 2013. A one-sided parliamentary election is scheduled to be held on next 5 January 2014, which has virtually divided the nation. Government took risk by deploying army in the whole country on last 26 December in aid to civil power. It can be said that if situation goes out of control of the government there is a chance to declare a State of Emergency. Actually, that will be the only option to overcome the deadlock as well as volatile situation.

Track record shows, every after emergency follows a change with difference. Bangladeshi people in home and abroad are in tension due to growing uncertainty. Ruling Awami League is going ahead desperately with the elections where 154 MP candidates have already been elected uncontested in absence of almost all opposition parties including main opposition BNP and its allies. The Government defied world's objections where UN, USA, EU, China, Japan and Commonwealth even Russia requested to stop this poll as it will not reflect the people's verdict and franchise while will fuel ongoing violence into a deep crisis. Army was deployed countrywide to assist election commission to hold elections in 59 districts out of 64 districts in the country. In all constituencies of the rest 5 districts, candidates were elected with understanding among ruling party and its alliances.

Trend of suppression and oppression which include mass arrest, detention, abduction and remand has been increased followed by the 'March for Democracy' of 29 December called by 18 Party Alliance and like-minded other political parties leader Khaleda Zia. Begum Zia is unofficially house arrest since she announced the programme 4 days before the programme. On the 29 December law enforcement agencies stopped Leader of the Opposition while she made an attempt to start for scheduled programme at her party office at Dhaka's Nayapaltan area by using her official car. She commented, "Parliament has not been dissolved yet and thereby I am still the Leader of the Opposition. How did you stop my movement?"

Institutions and organisations have been destroyed in Bangladesh over the years. Judiciary and Anti-Corruption Commission became government tools. Highly political people were appointed in non-political constitutional and government senior positions. Cases of ruling party were withdrawn by the government and opposition political parties cases remain. The government of the day became government of party in power instead of the people. Corruption has been encouraged by the government.

Stakeholders were not allowed to take part to decide how election will be held. Ruling party can decide within its tenure, but in Bangladesh now ruling party is deciding beyond their jurisdiction and tenure. Election is manipulated. Party in power pushes opposition political parties out of the election. They distribute parliamentary seats among them and their allies. They are violating the 'rules of game'. Mentionable, following fall of autocratic government in 1990, major political parties of Bangladesh agreed to hold election under non-party caretaker government in 1991 which was institutionalised in 1996. Since then all parliamentary elections have been held under non-party caretaker government. The last election was held in 29 December 2008 under a military-backed government which ruled the country for 2 years by overthrowing a constitutional caretaker government. Unfortunately, 2007-08 military-backed government was invited by the Awami League.

The illegitimate military government was also assured by them to be legitimised. BNP government was forced by Awami League to include the provision of Caretaker Government (CTG) in the constitution in 1996. Ironically, the same political party annulled the CTG provision constitutionally in 2011 as they came back to power after the gap of tenure. They could not repeal the constitution during their previous term of 1996-2001 as they did not have two-third majority to amend the constitution. Awami League has some other contradictions. The party staged movements with the support of Jamaat-e-Islami from 1994 to 1996 against BNP government and now they are pursuing trial against that party. Awami League struggled for democracy against army juntas during pre-independence period until 1971. Contrarily they invited the army to take over in number of times including 1982, 1990 and 2007. The AL used the driving force behind the army coup of 2007-08 and came to power. Al supported extra constitutional army-backed administration was not a caretaker government. Once they came to power, started attacking on CTG system instead, amended the constitution where the provision of CTG was annulled and trial of probable army coup was included. The fruit of much awaited separation of judiciary, which was completed by the last army government, is also being abused by present ruling party by placing their hardcore people. Besides, they replaced the provision of conducting the oath taking ceremony of President of the country by Speaker in place of Chief Justice. Awami League was against elections without major parties and going back to power they are now busy with the mockery, where repressing political agitations they are distributing parliamentary seats among themselves. Awami League was against authoritarian government and now they made their government one woman show. Previously also they switched over to Presidential system until was overthrown by bloody coup in 1975. Awami League replaced 'absolute trust and faith in almighty Allah' by secularism and they uphold 'Bismillahir Rahmanir Rahim' and State Religion Islam in the constitution. Same party was in the government for 5 years in 1996-2001 with all these above mentioned provision in the constitution. They signed 5 point treaty with Khelafat Majlish and did breach the agreement later. They also violated another treaty with Jatiya Party Chief by not appointing him the President. There were two more elections held in 1988 and 15 February 1996 which were not participated by all major parties. However, the election is due on 5 January is not compared with anyone held in the past as more than half of the seats were declared elected with understanding. This election is termed by opposition political parties and media as 'mockery with the nation'. For the first time no observers from home and abroad are coming to observe this election. Last time in 2007 EU declared that they will not observe the election although they came to Bangladesh for their mission as there was process of election finally boycotted by major parties. Meanwhile, that election could not be held.

Bangladesh Army did not allow then caretaker government in 2007 while another election was going on with the withdrawal by major opposition. Subsequently, country's power was captured by the army headed by then chief of staff Lt. General Moeen U ahmed, who was highly ambitious as well as determined to be the President. Serious violence has been taking place every day with number of deaths for about a month. UN Secretary General's Special Envoy Oscar Farnadez Taranco submitted some recommendations to the UN Secretary General in order to solve the Bangladesh crisis following his recent parley with the rival main political parties. Mr Taranco's submitted 4 points recommendations include 1. to solve political crisis by releasing opposition leaders immediately, allowing normal politics including keeping political parties offices open with political activities as such meeting, rally with creating congenial atmosphere, to replace Prime Minister by a neutral person by sending incumbent on leave and allocating Ministry of Public Administration and Home affairs to another two neutral persons during election time government. According to UN Special Envoy, if this solution does not work, the proposal prescribes: there will be election under UN system as such kind of polls held in other problematic countries in different times. If this also does not work, the last formulae is military action by deploying UN Peace Keeping Force in Bangladesh like Kongo, Sierra Leon, Sudan etc in order to hold parliamentary election under UN supervision following UN Charter 7.

Regarding ensuing parliamentary election, 21 registered political parties are away from election. Reportedly, a third biggest party is in a mess on the issue of participation in the polls. H M Ershad predicted that this election will not be held. UN Secretary General Ban Ki Moon and US Secretary of State John Kerry requested Prime Minister to stop the election. They recommended for a participatory election and end of violence in Bangladesh. Whole World backs UN. It is reported only India backs ruling Awami League in Bangladesh while America has been dealing with this. However, denying the allegation India recently issued a statement saying it does not want to interfere on internal affairs of Bangladesh. On the other hand, main opposition party BNP asked the Indian government to maintain relation with Bangladesh instead of maintaining exclusive relation with any particular political party.

Government used judiciary in annulling Caretaker Government system although Supreme Court gave opinion that next 2 parliamentary elections can be held under the CTG system. Before releasing the highest court's verdict government hurriedly changed the constitution's relevant provision. Besides, court has also its jurisdiction. Government has 3 organs namely Executive, Judiciary and Parliament and no one can cross its periphery. Politics should be dealt politically. It should be noted that what will be the system of the government and fundamentals of the constitution that will be decided by the politicians, not by the court. In other words, people's democratic rights can be ensured by the court, not to be curtailed. Apex court can interpret the constitution and if any fault happens through constitutional amendments that can be interpreted or corrected by the court. In 1988, Bangladesh Supreme Court annulled part of the 8th amendment of the constitution as it did not follow the unitary character of the constitution in respect to formation of 8 High Court Benches in divisional and greater district headquarters outside the capital. But, Supreme Court in recent verdict cancelled the provision of referendum on changing basic character of the constitution and they decided on fundamental issues of the constitution which is beyond their area. People are subject to decide what they want to follow and what not.

In our regime, following the BNP regime President Professor Dr Iajuddin Ahmed became head of caretaker government as the Chief Adviser. Initially AL did not want to accept him. I mediated between President and Awami League Chief Sheikh Hasina where we met all their demands including reshuffling the administration, sending Chief Election Commissioner (CEC) with some other Commissioners on leave etc. In present situation, Election Commission was appointed unilaterally by the government where party government headed by political Prime Minister remain. What an irony! The army is being used for party interest against the people.

Government deployed army in aid to civil power as we did so in our tenure which was made dysfunctional by Awami League on one hand and General Moeen and his associates on the other. That was followed by a State of emergency which I stopped for more than 3 months since October 2006 for the sake of democracy. Major political parties could not evaluate the gravity of the situation at that time. One party thought army chief will not betray since they appointed him superseding 9 senior officers following his lobbying for the post where he gave commitment to remain loyal if any odd situation arises. The other party was instigating the army to take over. However, due to chaos and anarchy, political support and army chief 's lust finally brought Bangladesh under a State of Emergency on 11 January 2007, which lead to a regime of an extra constitutional military-backed government that ruled the country for 2 years.

External interference is not acceptable if it is against the country. On the contrary, if external forces support any country for good cause then it is acceptable worldwide. For instance at the pressure of World Bank, Bangladesh adopted 'independent Anti-Corruption Commission bill' in the parliament in 2005 repealing formerly Anti-Corruption Board Act although later it was made useless organisation first by military rule and followed by civil regime. Similarly, under the pressure of donor countries and organisations number of Bangladesh's ministries was squeezed at that time. Although present government did reverse on this issue and in some cases increased even more. Examples are Food and Disaster Management Ministry, Children and Women Affairs Ministry and Railway Ministry. Prescription of donors is always not favourable for assistance recipient countries as under WB's pressure BNP government neglected the railway sector which went against Bangladesh as broadly considered. Considering the option, present AL government reversed the decision. Consequently, they created new ministry in this sector. It may be mentioned, India, China even Saudi Arbia are pursuing big projects in this sector as well.

During our time in 2006-07 UN, USA and allies were in favour of democracy as I made them understand. Later General Moeen sent an official request through an emissary to the USA State Department to allow him to declare Martial Law for a short period in order to make him the President. In this letter he promised, after becoming country's head of the State he will release all detainees, make country's political situation normal and will not dispute over any of two lady leaders to become the Prime Minister and Leader of the Opposition. Then that move proved my earlier appraisal to the international world was correct and timely. Meanwhile, the role of some foreign diplomats and some countries was controversial then. People's perception is more important in analysing the role of all actors. They evaluate both foreign and local actor's role independently and above any kind of interest. Presently Bangladeshi people are watching all internal and external actor's role very closely and international actor's role has been highly appreciated due to they want to save Bangladeshi democracy and its institutions and want to support them for further improvement.

Today's situation is worse than January 2007. Army leadership is one of the factors in taking over power. It depends on the army chief or some senior army officers whether they are ambitious. Government has taken a risk with deployment of army countrywide. At present, there are only few options left. If situation cannot be controlled, another State of emergency may be declared. Every after emergency follows either change of regime or military intervention. Previously that intervention brought martial law while new phenomenon shows that it brings military backed government. Example of last Martial Law and Military-backed Government occurred in 1982 and 2007 respectively both following State of Emergency. Army can act on its own or can wait for UN action. UN action can take some time as they need to go to UN General Assembly and Security Council. Regarding sending observers to the parliamentary election of Bangladesh lastly Russia supported USA as well. If government can hold the election and then gets some more time they will crack down on main opposition and there will be absence of check and balance.

This time government may overcome but at the end people will win in course of time and then it will be a great loss for Awami league. A democratic party may loss in one election while may come back in following polls. However, if it makes blunder it is deemed to be doomed. According to former President General Hussain Muhammad Ershad, who is an ally of present government, AL made everybody its enemy. He mentioned the recent incident where AL government attacked on Hefazat-e Islami, a non-political organisation as well.

General Ershad has been confined at Combined Military Hospital (CMH) for about a month as he does not want to support the AL government this time. AL came to power with JP's support twice.

There is no level playing field for all the political parties. Bangladesh has been practicing democracy on only one day which is on the day of election. Rest days of the tenure are far away from the people's rule. Only an election cannot help Bangladesh which needs total recast of the government machinery where system can work like developed countries. There must be a charter where all parties to agree. There should not be any dispute on basic or fundamental issues as for example values, religion, culture etc. As I have been witnessing governance of Bangladesh closely, I can draw a conclusion that the main problems of Bangladeshi politics are ego, mistrust, suspicion and discord. Right men are not rightly placed. In democracy there has to be compromise, not ego. Only living Nobel laureate of Bangladesh Dr Muhammad Yunus is being honoured worldwide while has been humiliated in his own country.

In the present political stalemate in Bangladesh, military takeover is not the solution. On the contrary, authoritarian government system must go and there should be checks and balances where all actors as well as organs should be accountable and transparent

Chapter 6

USA's Efforts For A New Election To Restore Democracy In Bangladesh

By M Mukhlesur Rahman Chowdhury

15 February 2014

Bangladesh is going to face impact of globalisation, which has real ground for that as well. This is because of recent one sided non-participatory parliamentary election held by the ruling party. The country has to face the world pressure to dissolve unaccepted parliament and hold a fresh election in the present era of globalisation. In particular, South Asia has been the world's attention, what was time and again disclosed by Obama administration, Chinese and Indian leaders. Consequently, one of the major countries of South Asia, Bangladesh has been struggling with democracy especially based on elections. Evidently, Bangladesh, as of South Asia, is in the centre point of this focus. It is obviously the country is heading towards unknown destination where government acts against the will of people as well as ignores United Nations and Western World. Bangladesh participates in UN peace keeping mission around the world whereas chaos and anarchy continues for a quite long time within the country. Eventually, the country cannot avoid effect of globalisation. Globalisation became a blessing for Bangladeshi people over the years, which is now a popular cause for western world as well. Moreover, recent political turmoil of Bangladesh has justified the external actor's intervention. Conversely, globalisation does not always work in the interest of people in various countries. Sometimes, it comes as challenge too.

In South Asia, the different countries have different problems. Sri Lanka and Nepal inherits ethnicity crises while Pakistan and Afghanistan have sectarian issues. On the other hand, India and Myanmar have been facing communal riots since long. Most of the South Asian nations belong to different caste, creed, tribes etc. In fact, the problem of Bangladesh is of a different attribute. Over time, Bangladeshi society has been developing as violent. It becomes highly politicised as well as intolerant. Only politics divides the nation.

With this in mind, it can easily be argued that, people of Bangladesh are quite different from its other neighbouring nations. They are neither fundamentalists nor fanatic. Instead, this homogenous nation is liberal and moderate what Islam, indeed, itself is. Despite continuous efforts of secularisation by a section of political parties and a group of society, without mandate of the people, Islam yet retains a strong political position in Bangladesh. Still it maintains as strong social bondage. Without understanding the characteristics of Bangladeshi people, it is really difficult to carry forward politics for this emerging nation in both home and abroad. Similarly while pursuing any research works on Bangladesh politics it needs to understand its people's value and ethos.

It will be very pertinent to mention here that since two decades, Mittelman (1994:429) argues, political globalisation centres on 'emerging worldwide preference for democracy'. Haynes (2005:11) echoed with him regarding this.

Regarding globalisation's impact on Bangladesh, we can find rationality from Jagdish Bhagwati's article titled "In Defence of Globalisation" (2010). Bhagwati (2010:526) argues in favour of his thoughts (here he mentioned lines) saying: "and so, while globalisation has a human face, can be made to glow yet better with appropriate governance along these lines. Globalisation works; but we can make it work better. That is the chief task before all of us today".

Haynes noted, "more recently, some comparative analyses of democratisation outcomes were more interested in the impact of external actors in both country-specific and regional organisations, such as the EU, not only proclaimed a general and theoretical commitment to encourage democracy around the world but also, in some cases, were able to back up their rhetoric with hard cash" (Haynes: 12).

What Fareed Zakaria (2010:220) discusses about some Arab countries is now applicable to Bangladesh. According to Zakaria, "they would happily come to power through an election, but then would set up their own theocratic rule. It would be one man, one vote, one time". It's dissimilarity in Bangladesh was recently occurred by the ruling party with a staged drama type 'election' without allowing opposition to participate by annulling Caretaker Government, detaining opponent political leaders, manipulating various government institutions especially judiciary and election commission and managing partisan administration, which yielded same result. In the recent Bangladeshi parliamentary election, 153 MPs were elected without any vote, the way the ruling party's position was secured. This was nothing but an election where ruling party would not be changed. Evidently, Caretaker Government (CTG) is justified for Bangladesh, which was established by present ruling party while they were in opposition to come to power. After coming back to power, this system became unnecessary thus obsolete to them. Hence, they annulled CTG system, what again shows similarity with Zakaria's argument.

Recently, UN Secretary General Ban Ki- Moon and his emissaries have already started working with their mission to Bangladesh. Subsequently, USA has taken some efforts to democratisation in Bangladesh. Obviously, it works under UN's initiative what is followed by other developed nations.

USA is one of the core components of United Nations (UN). Wherever, UN has taken action against any country USA played vital role. Like the world body, USA is pledge bound for democracy in home and abroad. Under the leadership of USA developed nations, in other words established democracies, are working together to hold an acceptable as well as credible election and democratise the existing faulty system of authoritarianism in Bangladesh.

Why USA to intervene in Bangladesh?

According to US State Department, Bangladesh is one of the major 'Moderate Muslim Role Model Countries'. Recently United States of America takes interest on Bangladesh. Strategically, Bangladesh stands at a very important position. As a result, USA, China and India's eyes are on Bangladesh. Before 1971 liberation war of Bangladesh, this nation has been under Indian hegemony both overtly and covertly. Most recently, based on a farcical parliamentary election in Bangladesh relations between USA and India turned into 'not good' (Prothom Alo 2014).

For instance, Bangladesh connects SAARC and ASEAN, bridging a divide between South Asia and South East Asia. Although Bangladesh is locked by India in its three sides, it has a window through Myanmar which reaches China through Kunming. Nonetheless, the country has a wider gateway (through waterway) at Bay of Bengal. Bangladesh established the SAARC to spread cooperation among South Asian nations, which inherits legacy of South Asia. Indeed, South Asia has a value. SAARC starts from Afghanistan to Sri Lanka. Arch rivals India and Pakistan have been escalating tensions through this regional organisation. Although SAARC represents one-fifth of world population, success of this regional body is little. Furthermore, the international world is keen to see progress of SAARC.

Concurrently, founder of Bangladesh Nationalist Party (BNP) former President of Bangladesh Ziaur Rahman has established absolute trust and faith in Allah and inserted 'Bismillahir Rahmanir Rahim' (Starting any deed in the name of Allah) in the beginning of constitution. Jatiya Party (JP) Chairman former President Hussain Muhammad Ershad has declared 'Islam' state religion. BNP led by its Chairperson Begun Khaleda Zia, wife of late President Zia, and her alliance continued following the above ideology. For obvious reason, secular political party Awami League (AL) declares before all elections from 1970 to 1973 led by the founding President of the country Sheikh Mujibur Rahman, during Pakistan period that, no law will be framed against Quran and Sunnah. The AL, led by Sheikh Hasina, daughter of late President Sheikh Mujib, pursued same policy with respect to its election pledge. On the eve of 2007 planned parliamentary elections AL signed 5 points treaty with Khelafat Majlish to implement Islamic laws and to annul anti-Islamic laws. Islam is considered as values, culture, identity and ethos in Bangladesh. This country is also champion of Asian values. Pakistan and Bangladesh became independent from British India based on Islam, which is way of life in this land. Pakistan remained Islamic Republic and Bangladesh inherits Islam as identity and deviated to People's Republic. Present Bangladesh was pioneer in establishing Pakistan in 1947. The Pakistan proposal (then it was called 'Lahore Proposal) was thrown by a Bangladeshi legendary leader A K Fazlul Huq (who was awarded title- 'Sher-e-Bangla', which means Tiger of Bengal for his brave role). Thus, Bangladesh bears three legacies. They are 'British legacy', 'Pakistani legacy' and a legacy of 'War of Secession'.

As I mentioned earlier about recent parliamentary election of Bangladesh, which held on last 5 January 2014, the whole world is well aware that this was a flawed election. However, why USA is interested to restore democracy in Bangladesh through a new election? On this much discussed issue, Sean M. Lynn-Jones noted: "After the cold war ended, promoting the international spread of democracy seemed poised to replace containment as the guiding principle of U.S. foreign policy. Scholars, policymakers, and commentators embraced the idea that democratisation could become America's next mission" (Lynn-Jones 1998).

According to the UN charter, "we the people's, reflect the fundamental principle of democracy that the will of the people is the source of legitimacy of sovereign states and therefore of the United Nations as a whole" (Democracy and United Nations). It may be mentioned that the World body (UN) plays role in fostering democracy through elections in respective countries. Under Secretary General for Political Affairs is designated by the General Assembly as the UN Focal Point for Electoral Assistance Activities. It has been seen in USA point of view that, "the international spread of democracy will offer many benefits to new democracies and to the United States" (Lynn-Jones 1998). Previously USA played role in African, Latin American and some European countries where the UN imposed sanctions, used UN troops or UN Peace Keeping Forces to solve political problems of many countries, including the Democratic Republic of Congo, Somalia, Sudan, Bosnia, Rwanda, Cambodia, Namibia, Haiti, Mozambique, Nicaragua, the former Yugoslavia, Syria and Sierra Leon. Against the backdrop of the prevailing volatile political situation in World focus South Asia's centre point Bangladesh opens gateway to end authoritarianism and foster democracy by Western World.

US Senate asked Bangladesh to hold a fresh election soon in its third hearing on last 11 February. Nisha Desai Biswal, US Assistant Secretary of State for South and Central Asian Affairs, US Ambassador to Bangladesh Dan W. Mozena commented: relations between Bangladesh and America are not normal. Besides, USA is sending a team to assert on this issue. Canada, Australia, the Netherlands, China, Germany, UK are, among others, pursuing on this issue very seriously in line with America's mission. Bangladesh faces problem with USA on GSP issue. USA most recently stopped training facilities for Rapid Action Battalion (RAB) due to gross violation of human rights has been committing by this force. In the context of globalisation, World Bank closed one of the biggest projects in Bangladesh namely Padma Bridge for reported corruption, where Canada police intercepted it and conducting the investigation. WB was followed by International Monetary Fund (IIMF), Asian Development Bank (ADB), Islamic Development Bank (IDB) and Japan.

Following the hearing of the US Senate Committee, as Nisha Desai briefed the media:

"On January 5, the government held a deeply flawed election in which one of the two major political parties did not participate. As a result, over half of the 300 members of parliament were elected unopposed, and most of the rest faced only token opposition. The election did not credibly express the will of the Bangladeshi people. This could have serious ramifications for stability in Bangladesh and the region".

The US spokesman further added:

"Immediately after the election, we issued a strong statement noting that the election was not a credible reflection of the will of the people and called for immediate dialogue to agree on new elections as soon as possible."

US Senate passed another resolution on Bangladesh 11 December, 2013. US Ambassador recently reported to his government while he was in his country on both leave and official tour and he has been engaged to go ahead with US's mission of democratisation in Bangladesh.

During the week of December 8, 2013, United Nations Assistant Secretary General Oscar Fernandez-Taranco visited Bangladesh to foster political dialogue between Bangladeshi political parties and leaders in order to bring a halt to violence and allow for a credible peaceful election.

Similarly, UK House of Commons has also arranged three hearing on Bangladesh issue. Canada and Australia are also following the same. Commonwealth issued official letter to Bangladesh government regarding this. EU's position has not been changed like USA. These are all the result of globalising world.

Flashback: The role of UN and USA in 2007

USA helped in continuing democratic practice during our governance. Lieutenant General Moeen U Ahmed wanted to declare martial law by 12 January 2007. I sought help from both UN and USA to stop that military intervention. US Ambassador Patricia A. Butenis extended whole hearted cooperation in this regard. We used to meet regularly those days, sometimes at my office at "Bangabhaban" and sometimes at her official residence at Gulshan's "Habib Villa" in Dhaka, the capital of Bangladesh. Butenis was saying me one day: "although you are doing many good deeds for the sake of democracy, however, you need to do something visible". Evidently, when she saw that I have compromised a lot for continuity of democracy, she connected me to US State Department. One fine morning, Under Secretary of State of USA Nicholas Burns called me. US Assistant Secretary of State for Public Affairs in the Department of State Richard A. Boucher spoke with me to my mobile phone and also spoke with President Professor Dr. Iajuddin Ahmed to the same cell phone through me. My relations with the UN Secretary General Kofi A. Annan also worked. He sent a small but important delegation led by his special envoy Craig Gennes. On the other hand, following our parley Richard Boucher visited Bangladesh with a US delegation. Similarly, we had contact with Secretary of State of USA Condoleezza Rice as well. The role of some diplomats' was mysterious and some other played dubious role whereas most of them were managed by Butenis. There was a diplomatic club called 'Tuesday Group'. UN Resident Representative Reanata Lok Dessallien's role was controversial. Lt. General Moeen availed this advantage. Although Renata made her position clear when she completed her assignment to Bangladesh as UN Resident Coordinator that she did not support Moeen (Ittefaq 2011; Daily Star 2011), but by the time situation would be compared as 'the patient had died before the doctor came'. Canadian High Commissioner Barbara Richardson's attitude was not right. Australian High Commissioner Douglas Fosket told me once that "we used to discuss about you as you are the main contact point of the government. We do appreciate your role for your country. On our behalf Butenis maintains contact with you".

There was a negative perception about the then British High Commissioner Anwar Choudhury, who used to speak much. Butenis told me, "Don't worry. I will manage him". I convinced UN and US led different countries diplomats thus international world that martial law is going to be declared soon. At one stage, India had to tell Moeen that if America does not support, it will be difficult for India to help any army rule in the unipolar world with globalisation context.

On 7 January 2007, I sent a copy to top politicians what I received from Counter Intelligence of Directorate General of Forces Intelligent (DGFI), which echoed my prediction and analysis that by 12 January there will be a martial law in Bangladesh. Concerned politicians did not believe it (Daily Sun 2013). However, UN and USA categorically informed Bangladesh military leaders about their three points' formulae in regard to any probable military coup. They were: 1. martial law will not be accepted, 2. if martial law is declared in Bangladesh, all Bangladeshi peace keepers in UN will be back and 3. there will be sanctions imposed on the country if this is the situation. Then army chief went back to his original option of State of Emergency (henceforth emergency), which was already supported by both parties' top leaders, knowingly or unknowingly, which can be termed as 'marriage of convenience'. One party supported emergency by understanding and other one without understanding. I stopped it since 29 October 2006, the following day of much talked 'Logi-Boitha' event (Thikana 2008; Bangla Times 2010).

When Military leaders declared a State of Emergency, I contacted with US government. Butenis informed me that martial law was stopped. But, it is not possible to stop State of Emergency as Bangladesh constitution allows President to declare it. I said President is under gun point and then I was replied if this is the case, we should be told by the President officially. Following declaration of emergency, Moeen sent a designated army officer of DGFI to US State Department seeking US support for short period of martial law if necessary for three months and if not possible for even only one day in order to make army chief Moeen President and promised, after that everything will be as usual. He would not mind if one becomes Prime Minister and other one Leader of the Opposition. US administration outright rejected the proposal saying what Presidential Adviser Mukhlesur Rahman Chowdhury predicted earlier on this, now it has been proved. USA did not only turn down the proposal of martial law, but also asked to hand over power to politicians after holding parliamentary elections as soon as possible (Budhbar 2009; ManabZamin 2009; Amader Shomoy 2009). Finally, Bangladesh could escape probable pro-longed third military regime through effect of globalisation.

Now in changed scenario, according to UN Charter, the world body asks Bangladesh government to hold a fresh election by dissolving the present unaccepted one, if this formula does not work then UN will organise a fresh election under its supervision comprising election experts from its different member countries and if this also does not accepted by the government, in that case UN will use its troops of UN Peace Keeping Mission and drive a cleansing programme in political field and hold elections (Chowdhury 2013; Chowdhury 2014). If the mission exercises until to the last, it will cost a lot for the country like Bangladesh and if discord continues eventually there may be a reform programme for the Bangladeshi organisations and institutions, which will not be good for politicians and political parties. Obviously government should take responsibility and protect the country by arranging a new parliamentary election and also by arranging programmes of good governance.

This is the era of globalisation and we can come to a conclusion "that a key effect of globalisation is to increase the porousness of state boarders and to enhance the significance of external actors for many domestic outcomes" (Hay 2005:3). As a result, Bangladesh cannot avoid world's pressure to dissolve unaccepted parliament and will have to organise a new parliamentary election, which is obviously a manifestation in favour of mass people of Bangladesh. The sooner the government of Bangladesh understands this reality, the better for the country and its people.

M Mukhlesur Rahman Chowdhury is a London-based Researcher as well as Independent Analyst in Politics and International Relations. A Career Journalist Mukhles Chowdhury is a Former Minister and Adviser to the President of Bangladesh. Former President of Overseas Correspondents' Association Bangladesh (OCAB) Mukhles Chowdhury has been working as the Chief Editor of the Bangladesh Worldwide and the Weekly Prekshit as well. Email: **mukhleschow@gmail.com**

References

Amader Shomoy, 2009. Dhaka, Bangladesh
Bangla Times, 2010. London, UK
Bhagwati, J. 2010, In Defence of Globalisation, Essential Readings in Comparative Politics, W.W. North & Company New York. London
Budhbar, 2009. Dhaka, Bangladesh
Daily Star, 2011. Dhaka, Bangladesh
Daily Sun, 2013. Dhaka, Bangladesh
Haynes, J. 2005, Comparative Politics in a Globalising World, Page 3, Polity Press, Cambridge, UK
Haynes, J. 2005, Comparative Politics in a Globalising World, Page 11-12, Polity Press, Cambridge, UK
Lynn-Jones, S. 1998, "Why the United States Should Spread Democracy" Discussion Paper 98-07, Centre for Science and International Affairs, Harvard University.
ManabZamin, 2009. Dhaka, Bangladesh
Mittelman (1994:429), Comparative Politics in a Globalising World, Page 11, Polity Press, Cambridge, UK
Prothom Alo, 2014. Dhaka, Bangladesh
Thikana, 2008. New York, USA
Zakaria, F. 2010, Islam, Democracy, and Constitutional Liberalism, Essential Readings in Comparative Politics, W.W. North & Company New York. London

Table of Contents

Printed by Books on Demand GmbH, Norderstedt / Germany